THE 1975 PORTLAND TIMBERS

THE BIRTH OF SOCCER CITY, USA

MICHAEL ORR

Charleston | London

THE
History
PRESS

Published by The History Press
Charleston, SC 29403
www.historypress.net

Cover: Portland Timbers properties courtesy of Major League Soccer, LLC.

First published 2012

Manufactured in the United States

ISBN 978.1.60949.466.7

Library of Congress Cataloging-in-Publication Data

Orr, Michael.
The 1975 Portland Timbers : the birth of soccer city, USA / Michael Orr.
p. cm.
Includes index.
ISBN 978-1-60949-466-7
1. Portland Timbers (Soccer team)--History. 2. Soccer teams--Oregon--Portland.
I. Title. II. Title: Nineteen seventy five Timbers.
GV943.6.P58O77 2012
796.33409795'49--dc23
2011045620

For Morgen

whom I cannot live without

Contents

Acknowledgements   7
Introduction   9

1. Oregon Soccer, Inc., and the North American Soccer League   11
2. Introductions in the Locker Room   28
3. Willie Anderson and the 4-3-3   38
4. The Winning Streak   50
5. Four Games in Nine Days   71
6. Top of the Table   89
7. Do You Know the Way to San Jose?   100
8. The Portland Timbers   112

Notes   117
Bibliography   121
Index   123
About the Author   128

Acknowledgements

This book would have been impossible to conceive without the contributions in time, resources and patience from dozens of individuals across Portland, the United States and, indeed, the world.

Willie Anderson, Tony Betts, Graham Brown, Don Cox, Leo Crowther, Gisele Currier, Chris Dangerfield, Scott Daniels, Graham Day, Art Dixon, Bernie Fagan, Terry Fisher, Roger Goldingay, Linda and Mick Hoban, Vic Karsner, Jimmy Kelly, Dave Landry, Ray Martin, Nick Nicolas, Dennis O'Meara, John Polis, Barry Powell, Augusto and Beatriz Proaño, Jim Rilatt, Kurt Schubothe, Gary St. Clair, Dave Stoops, Jim Taylor, Stella Terry, David Tossell, Bob Wilmot and Peter Withe were all willing to chat with me, from brief notes to hours-long conversations. Their memories are the backbone of this book.

Jim Brown, David Instone, Bill Lodey and Matt Young helped me locate former players living in Great Britain. Val Ballestrem, Michael Cox, Scott Daniels and Geoff Wexler, Lauren Drury and Mike Rose, Abram Goldman-Armstrong, Mary Hansen, Dave Morrison, the Multnomah County Library, Dave Wasser and Jonathan Wilson were extremely helpful with research inquiries.

Special thanks is due to Kevin Alexander, John Bain, Josh Barrett, Eric Berg, Brian Costello, Jim Cumbes, Joe Elsmore, Mike Golub, Bill Irwin, Marsha Matthews, Scott McLaren-Moreton, Harry Merlo, Sean Moran, Ann Nolan, Fernando Proaño, Robby Robinson, Jim Serrill and Kathy Smith for their assistance in many different ways throughout the life of this and related projects. And thanks to Aubrie Koenig at The History Press for talking me through the process of turning tens of thousands of words into a published book.

The Portland Timbers have been nothing but supportive of this endeavor. In meetings, conversations and correspondence they have always been open and encouraging.

As a member of FC Media, I thank Matthew Speakman and Morgen Young, as well as Steven Lenhart, for their invaluable contributions. This book was born in a Portland apartment in the summer of 2009 and has been completed only through teamwork and persistence. Without the combined efforts of FC Media, there would be no book.

And I especially thank my wife, Morgen, for supporting me with this project and my obsession with it. Beyond her listening, reading and editing, she gave me the confidence to keep writing and gave up many hours and evenings that could have been spent doing something more fun. That this has turned into a book is owed to her, and I hope she's as proud of it as I am of her work.

Introduction

On August 14, 1975, Portlanders arrived at Civic Stadium in the heart of the west side of the city. By 4:00 a.m., a line stretched southward from the ticket windows at the corner of Southwest Morrison Street and Twentieth Avenue, nearly to Southwest Taylor Street and the Bullpen Bar. Come daylight, thousands of residents of the Rose City were wrapped clear around the stadium, waiting for the chance to buy a ticket to the most anticipated sporting event in Portland's professional sporting history.

With sixty-seven seasons of minor-league baseball in Portland, an out-of-town passerby might have expected the long lines to be for a baseball game of some import. But everyone in Portland knew exactly what would take place at Civic Stadium on August 17: the Portland Timbers soccer team was hosting a North American Soccer League (NASL) semifinal against the St. Louis Stars. Despite heavy rains and lines that seemed stagnant, 33,503 Portlanders passed through the gates at Civic Stadium that day, forging the second-largest crowd in NASL history to that point.

Outfitted in plastic ponchos, the overflow crowd stomped in unison, passed their buckets of beer and cheered on their beloved Timbers. City councilwoman Mildred Schwab had arranged for every spare set of bleachers in town to be stationed as close to the pitch as possible, creating a deafening roar as the Timbers waded through deep puddles on the Tartan turf surface. St. Louis's goalkeeper, Peter Bonetti, England's World Cup starter in 1970, was peppered with twenty-eight shots and nineteen corner kicks. A driving kick from midfielder Barry Powell found defender Graham Day, who flicked

1975 Portland Timbers official team picture. *Courtesy of Tony Betts, personal collection.*

a perfectly placed ball to the head of Peter Withe, Portland's center forward. Withe's nod had Bonetti well beaten and gave Portland all it would need to advance to Soccer Bowl '75, the pinnacle of soccer in the United States.

The sopping throngs were delirious as their magical summer came to a close, sending their boys to San Jose to contest the NASL's championship game. That scene could hardly have been imagined just four months earlier when fourteen British footballers arrived in Oregon for the inaugural season of a club called the Portland Timbers. With each passing month, soccer became more important and an event of civic consequence. The story of the original seventeen players and two coaches is the story of Portland—an experience in hard work, friendship, tolerance and achievement. Their story is one that must never be forgotten in Soccer City, USA, for all future Timbers owe that very status to the pioneers who so ably took the pitch in the summer of 1975.

Oregon Soccer, Inc., and the North American Soccer League

Major professional soccer came to North America in 1967 in the form of two leagues: the United Soccer Association (USA), which brought entire foreign clubs to North America to play a summer schedule, and the National Professional Soccer League (NPSL). With clubs playing across the continent, from the southeastern United States to Canadian British Columbia, the USA and NPSL brought professional soccer to markets where it had rarely, if ever, been found before. Prior to the 1968 season, the two leagues merged, resulting in the North American Soccer League and the start of a sixteen-year presence on the continent.

By late 1974, the NASL had grown to fifteen teams after the folding of the Atlanta Apollos and Montréal Olympique and the admission of eight new clubs: Baltimore Comets, Boston Minutemen, Denver Dynamos, Los Angeles Aztecs, San Jose Earthquakes, Seattle Sounders, Vancouver Whitecaps and Washington Diplomats. The westward push of the young league was a clear objective of commissioner Phil Woosnam. Woosnam was a veteran of West Ham United and Aston Villa in the professional ranks in England, as well as a Welsh international prior to his move stateside in 1966. He was player-coach with the Atlanta Chiefs in the earliest days of the NASL and coached the United States national team in 1968. In 1973, the NASL featured just nine clubs, none farther west than Dallas, so a major westward expansion was an exploratory step in the evolution of America's top-flight league.

By the end of the 1974 season, Los Angeles was champion, while San Jose, Seattle and Vancouver all drew huge crowds to their games. A visitor to one such game was Don Paul, a former Pro Bowl defensive back for the Cleveland Browns and two-time NFL champion. Paul, a native of Tacoma, Washington, was director of player personnel for the World Football League's Portland Storm in 1974. The Storm went 7-12-1 in their first and only season before the IRS impounded the club. Disillusioned with the failure of the Storm, Paul traveled north to his family's home in Tacoma. According to John Gilbertson, a Portland lawyer, "Don was visiting his mother when he went to a soccer game. He liked what he saw, and he showed me some financial statements which looked sound to me." Those financial statements made sense because of the tremendous home support garnered by Seattle and, to an even greater extent, San Jose. The two new clubs led the league in average attendance, with the Sounders reaching 13,500 and the Earthquakes topping 16,000 per game, compared to a league average of 7,825. With Seattle owner Walt Daggatt claiming the Sounders' return of 90 percent of investment through ticket sales and the possibility of playing in a twenty-seven-thousand-seat stadium in Portland, Paul convinced Gilbertson that soccer was the sport for Portlanders to focus on. The two quickly founded Oregon Soccer, Inc. (OSI), in the hopes of attracting investment toward the NASL's $100,000 franchise fee.

Visits from Daggatt and Lamar Hunt, the influential owner of the NASL's Dallas Tornado, in the fall of 1974 solidified Portland's status as a potential site to fill the space between Seattle and San Jose. With the NASL expected to expand further in 1975, the West Coast clubs were looking for at least one more to join their ranks and ease the increasingly distant travel schedule. Paul also aimed to have investment in the Portland soccer club come directly from Oregonians, keeping the focus local and actively engaging the community in the affairs of the team.

Due to OSI's late start in filing its registration with the Oregon Corporation Commission, the fledgling group was not able to file an official application with the NASL in time to attend October meetings in Texas. The league had already accepted bids from Tampa and San Antonio for new clubs, and Chicago was expected to fill the third of five openings. Additional meetings in mid-November were considered the likely date for the official inclusion of Portland into the NASL.

Instead, three months followed without an announcement. By Christmas, OSI had sold $75,000 in shares at $1,000 each and had another $100,000 pledged toward its efforts. Though the fundraising was impressive given the exclusively local nature of investment, the cash in hand was far short of the required $350,000 needed to cover franchise fees, first-year operating expenses and additional working capital. OSI president John Gilbertson still expected Portland and Hartford to occupy the final two of the NASL's proposed twenty-team league in 1975, but time was running very short with the season due to begin as early as late April.

Adding a twentieth club would make the NASL the third largest in North America at the time, trailing only the National Football League's twenty-six and Major League Baseball's twenty-four. Despite OSI's struggles to raise the necessary funds throughout the fall of 1974, Phil Woosnam was willing to work with John Gilbertson and Don Paul to extend deadlines to get Portland into the league. With steadily increasing attendance, from a league-wide average of 3,844 per game in 1971 to 7,825 in 1974, and a television contract for select games on CBS, Woosnam was confident that even a last-minute deal in Portland could continue the strong growth of the NASL, particularly in the swelling Northwest.

The first week of the New Year saw significant changes in the status of Portland as a potential site for NASL expansion. With the Rose City and Hartford judged to be the most viable options for the remaining two expansion slots, Woosnam, Lamar Hunt and San Jose general manager Dick Berg visited for emergency meetings to determine the financial position of Portland's bid. Two days of meetings revealed that OSI was still roughly $90,000 short of the necessary funding. Yet the league, in its quest to have an even number of teams and a full twenty, officially offered a franchise to the Portland group, contingent on its completing fundraising by January 13. By January 20, the league was again delaying its confirmation of a club in Portland due to a lack of funding and legal requirements. Hartford was named the NASL's nineteenth team on January 21, leaving only Portland to fill the four-division league.

With the league pushing for an agreement but without full financial commitment locally, Oregon Soccer, Inc., considered waiting until the 1976 season for a Portland franchise. But with fears that the league could increase the franchise and operating fees from $350,000 to near $1 million in the next calendar year, OSI made one final, desperate push to secure financing. This was doubly necessary as Woosnam soon warned OSI that 1975 was the final year the league would accept a bid from Portland. Only major television markets would be sought moving forward, and with Portland ranking as the twenty-fifth largest market in the United States, the time had come to put up the remaining money or abandon the plan of soccer in the Rose City. With John Gilbertson out of town, Don Paul received a phone call from Lamar Hunt insisting that OSI post the required funds or lose the proposed franchise. OSI reached across the Columbia River for the first time, contacting longtime youth coach Augusto "Doc" Proaño in nearby Vancouver, Washington. Though the goal had always been to secure complete investment from within Portland itself, the desperation of the looming deadline had Paul calling Proaño, who was on vacation in Las Vegas. Ahead of the 5:00 p.m. deadline, an unnamed investor assured Paul that the remaining money would be in the bank by the final of many deadlines. At the end of the business day, Paul was able to call Phil Woosnam with the good news: Portland had raised the necessary money and was ready to join the NASL.

On January 23, 1975, the league officially awarded Portland its twentieth franchise. Portland was nestled into the Western Division alongside Vancouver, Seattle, San Jose and Los Angeles. From the beginning, Paul aimed to intimately involve his players and coaches in the community. "They'll do it because they are unique, and we'll select them on personality as well as ability," Paul said of his future team. Though he had only been in Portland a short time, the OSI vice-president was keenly aware of the close-knit community in the Rose City. By selling the club from its earliest days as one committed to that community, Paul hoped to attract fans before the team set foot on the pitch.

Having drawn the admission process to its boiling point, the new soccer club had missed its chance to take part in the NASL's annual collegiate draft. While Paul claimed not to be worried by the failure to organize quickly enough to immediately introduce young American players, the facts facing the new club were glaring. With three months before the start of the season, the Portland club had neither a coach nor players. Portland would have to find a manager, likely one with European connections, in order to find enough players to fill out the eighteen-man roster required by the NASL. Paul immediately set his eyes toward England, hoping to reduce the language barrier.

Freddie Goodwin,[1] Gordon Jago and Vic Crowe were the managers interviewed in Portland. Jago had been the USA manager in 1969, replacing Woosnam when the latter moved to the NASL's top job. Jago had the distinction of having played in the NASL with the Baltimore Bays but also came to OSI as a manager of some repute in the lower divisions in London. Goodwin managed the New York Generals in the NPSL from 1967 to 1968, and by 1975 he was rounding out his fifth season at Birmingham City. Crowe had been captain for five of his twelve years at Aston Villa and won sixteen caps for Wales. His playing career led him to three seasons with the Atlanta Chiefs in the NASL, including his team's MVP award, and a league championship under Woosnam in 1967. In 1969, he moved back home to manage his club, Aston Villa, for more than four years but was sacked in 1974.

Initially, Jago was the leading candidate for the job in Portland. OSI was determined to name a manager as soon as possible and was working with Millwall to buy Jago out of his contract. But through the late winter, Gilbertson and Paul were unable to convince Millwall that their manager should leave after less than one season. With Jago unavailable, the Portland club focused their attention on Crowe.[2] Being without a club for almost a year had its advantages for Crowe, giving him the ability to begin work immediately without the consent of another club. Crowe was announced as the first Portland manager on March 6, 1975. "He plays a very fast and aggressive game. This is the kind of soccer we want. Vic has assured us he's planning an offense-oriented type of team," said Paul in announcing Crowe.

Crowe was named manager of a club without a name. The NASL had awarded the city a club in January, and the club had completed a coaching search just two months before the start of the season. Yet the potential supporters of the club had to keep waiting for the team's nickname. Earlier in the year, OSI had sent ballots requesting naming suggestions from Oregonians across the state with a deadline of March 5. Prizes were promised to those who suggested the winner, including a road trip with the team. When Crowe was hired, Gilbertson, Paul and company counted the votes and realized they had a problem: the winning name, by a wide margin, was Portland Pioneers. Of the 3,000 votes collected, 157 chose Pioneers. The name was historically appropriate, referencing the famous Oregon Trail and the pioneers who came to Oregon in the nineteenth century. But nearby Lewis and Clark College was also nicknamed the Pioneers, leaving either a trademark issue or local confusion. Instead of fighting for the official, though unannounced, winner, OSI moved to the second-most popular name on its list: Timbers. Other discarded suggestions included Pride, RainDrops, Steelheads, Columbians and Volcanoes.

On March 8, 1975, the Portland Timbers were born. All that stood between the Portland Timbers and their inaugural NASL game was a squad of players. With that in mind, Vic Crowe set out for England, immediately returning to his old city and club to begin the process of recruiting players to join his team for the summer of '75.

Upon his return to England in mid-March, Crowe employed Leo Crowther, an old friend from Aston Villa, to help attract players to the

Portland Timbers and work out the details with their home clubs. Crowe and Crowther scoured the country for players whom they thought would fit into both the league and city profiles. Never mind that Crowther had never stepped foot in Portland and Crowe had spent just a few days in the Rose City. Crowther had been the youth team manager at Aston Villa and was known as a successful manager of younger players as Villa won the FA Youth Cup in 1972. The two men with deep connections to the West Midlands region of England set out in familiar surroundings, tapping the Villa straight away.

While Crowe and Crowther were recruiting players in England, the Timbers began their formal sale of season tickets on March 21. Without players to advertise and barely a coach and nickname involved, the club managed to field orders for 512 season tickets before the drive even began. Only six weeks stood between the opening of ticket sales and the Timbers' first game, officially slated for May 2 at home against the Seattle Sounders. Ticket prices were set at five dollars or less, and family packages were available for eight dollars. Paul was hopeful that the central location of Civic Stadium, the proposed host of the Timbers; the ease of accessibility by bus; and the affordable ticket prices would attract more than enough fans to support the club and perhaps even keep it from losing money. But before the masses could convert to soccer fans, the Timbers needed at least one face in town to inspire the Rose City.

"Support the Portland Timbers," read the advertisement on page C6 of the Sunday, March 23, 1975 edition of the *Oregonian* newspaper. The advert was the first public display of the new logo developed by the Timbers. "The Portland logo was designed to be round to mimic the shape of a soccer ball; the axe was a manifestation of a prominent industry in the Northwest; the chevrons were a stylized version of a tree," says Dennis O'Meara, the club's twenty-three-year-old public relations director in 1975. Though the ad in the newspaper was black-and-white, the Timbers had also selected their color scheme for the coming season with the help of Gerber Advertising Agency. With Oregon's trees so

1975 Portland Timbers pocket schedule featuring the original logo. Without much time or budget in their first season, the Timbers released simple items for fans. *Courtesy of Nick Nicolas.*

explicitly used in name and hinted at in design, green was an obvious choice for the Timbers. Somewhat controversially, the club chose old gold as a secondary color, edging quite close to the University of Oregon's green and yellow base. "There was a lot of other preliminary work to get done before the season started with a front office staff of just five people," O'Meara remembers. "So the nickname and team colors were not debated very long."

BRIAN GODFREY AND MICHAEL HOBAN had little in common before the early spring of 1975. Both spent time at Aston Villa until 1971, when they moved on from Villa Park. Godfrey had captained Villa in the League Cup final against Tottenham Hotspur in 1971. Hoban was in the reserve team. Godfrey moved to Bristol Rovers with 348 football league matches and 98 goals to his name. Hoban had never appeared with the first team at Villa in a league match. Godfrey had won three caps for Wales. Hoban had won a cap with the U.S. national team in 1973. When Godfrey left Villa, he played another 199 games at Bristol Rovers and Newport County. Hoban spent the early '70s with the Atlanta Chiefs and Denver Dynamos of the NASL. Yet their different backgrounds came together on March 25, 1975, when Vic Crowe signed them as the first Portland Timbers.

Crowe signed Brian Godfrey because he was an aggressive player with the experience necessary to lead the team. As a fellow Welshman and the captain at Villa under Crowe earlier in the decade, Godfrey was Crowe's chosen leader. "Brian Godfrey was the epitome of Vic on the field. You could replace one with the other. Brian was tough and uncompromising but a very talented player, too," says Mick Hoban. Of Godfrey, Crowe remarked, "He was my captain when we were together at Aston Villa, and he's my captain here."

Hoban was brought into Portland for very different reasons. As a young defender with experience in the NASL, Hoban was the Timbers' ambassador and first on the ground in Portland. Arriving on April 10, the defender came to be one of the Timbers' most significant signings. His young age belied his experience in the business world of American professional soccer. In both previous NASL cities, Hoban had served as community liaison, helping his teammates in their acclimation to life stateside. He was captain of Atlanta at age twenty and was simultaneously the club's business manager. Hoban signed with Crowe and the Timbers knowing he would be the initial link between his future teammates and the Portland community.

Says Hoban, "I worked with the front office, in terms of promotions and community, doing various things like finding apartments for when the

Jan Gilbertson, Don Paul, Mick and Linda Hoban, John Gilbertson and Lucile Paul sharing a drink prior to the arrival of the other sixteen Timbers. The Hobans were the first to arrive in Portland and were given the Gilbertsons as their host family. *Courtesy of Mick Hoban, personal collection.*

players arrived, transportation and what the families would need. Linda and I worked with the Gilbertsons because they were our initial point of contact, as well as Don Paul and Dennis O'Meara. We worked our way around the community and made appearances, trying to spread the word." Portland was the third stop in America for Hoban, so the process of learning a community, both as a team and as a family, was familiar.

While Godfrey and Hoban prepared to join the new Portland Timbers, Crowe and Crowther moved ahead securing a workable squad. The Timbers had a central midfielder as well as a young defender. The two Villa men knew that both players and clubs would have to be convinced that a summer in America was a good idea and that they would need a mixture of skill and experience. Crowther found that most clubs were more than happy to lighten their summer wage bills, so emphasis could be put on acquiring exactly the type of players the Timbers' coaches wanted. "We decided that we would approach clubs who had first team quality men in their reserve sides, young players whom we had at Villa and an experienced keeper," describes Crowther.

By April 1, Crowe announced, by phone, that he had his eye on as many as ten new players for the inaugural Timbers' squad. Though he would not name the players until the necessary paperwork was complete, he assured Don Paul that his team would bring players from England's First Division and blend youth with experience. The season was looming just four weeks away, leaving Paul concerned that a lack of cohesion could make the early part of the season difficult. "So many of the teams are already playing exhibitions, and we won't even have our first players in town for another couple of weeks," Paul worried.

Having convinced the British government that his selected players were eligible for a special visa, Crowe finally released the names of nine new signings on April 7. Five players came from the First Division, three were twenty-one years old or younger and three were at least twenty-eight years old. In short, Crowe found exactly the types of players he said he would.

The nine players helped assuage Paul's fears of a team of strangers. Four of the new players came from the Wolverhampton Wanderers, all between nineteen and twenty-three years old. One player came from Birmingham City, and two more were formerly with Aston Villa. In all, seven of the nine had played within a twenty-mile radius over the previous decade, some as teammates and some as local rivals in the West Midlands.

Overnight the Portland Timbers grew from two players to eleven, meaning regardless of what else happened, the club could at least field a team on May 2 against Seattle. The four new players from the Wolves were Jimmy Kelly, a twenty-one-year-old winger from Northern Ireland; Englishmen Peter Withe, a twenty-three-year-old striker; England U23 international Barry Powell, a twenty-one-year-old midfielder; and Chris Dangerfield, a nineteen-year-old forward and a member of the Wolves' reserve side. Birmingham City provided Ray Martin, a thirty-year-old defender with thirteen seasons and three hundred games' experience. Two former Aston Villa players joined the Timbers from other clubs, with twenty-eight-year-old winger Willie Anderson signing on loan from Cardiff City of the Second Division and Barry Lynch, a twenty-four-year-old defender with NASL experience with the Atlanta Chiefs. Anderson had been a star at Villa but had started his career with Manchester United in the mid-'60s. Portland drew twenty-nine-year-old goalkeeper Graham Brown from the Doncaster Rovers, a Fourth Division side, and Tommy McLaren, a twenty-five-year-old Scotsman who was already an established presence at Port Vale in the Fourth Division.

The NASL maximum for roster size for the 1975 season was eighteen players. By mid-April, the Timbers had eleven to their name, with Crowe and Crowther still searching clubs for three more players. On April 18, just two weeks ahead of the debut game, Crowe signed his final English players. Donald Gardner, born in Jamaica but raised in England, joined from Wolverhampton as a nineteen-year-old forward. Gardner marked the sixth First Division player to join the Timbers, five of them coming from the Wolves, giving Portland the highest such total in the NASL. Graham Day, a twenty-one-year-old defender from Bristol Rovers, joined Hoban, Lynch and Martin at the back, while Tony Betts, a twenty-one-year-old at Aston Villa, joined the forward line. Their work in England complete, Crowe and Crowther made plans to return to Portland to prepare for the start of the season. Crowe departed immediately, arriving in the Rose City on April 22. Crowther stayed behind to corral the players who would be making the move to America.

Of all the planning, scheduling and adjusting Vic Crowe would need to accomplish in the ten days leading to his club's first game, his first task in Portland was to conduct a two-day tryout of American players. With a league requirement of three players with North American citizenship for 1975's expansion teams, Crowe had to find at least three worthy of inclusion in the first team. Having spent nearly every day of his time employed as

1973–74 Wolverhampton Wanderers official reserve team photo. Four players joined the Timbers in 1975, including Barry Powell (top row, second from right), Chris Dangerfield (middle row, second from left), Donald Gardner (middle row, far right) and Jimmy Kelly (bottom row, far right). *Courtesy of Chris Dangerfield, personal collection.*

Timbers manager finding and convincing players in England to come to America, the mandated triumvirate stood as an obstacle and annoyance for Crowe. The club hoped to have at least several newly minted Timbers arrive from England and join the tryouts to better gauge how the North American players could compete and react with English veterans. But trouble with immigration prevented all but Mick Hoban from attending.

"I think we may find a couple who can help us," was about all Crowe could muster after cutting the field of sixty down to twenty-one after the first day. Yet Hoban, more recently involved in American soccer than Crowe, thought, "It is a lot better group than we had a year ago at Denver." Crowe had his eyes on several players in particular, chiefly those who had played professionally, with preferential treatment toward those with NASL experience. Nick Nicolas came north from the San Jose Earthquakes' free agent team, Rino Augustino played on the Toronto Metros' free agent side in 1974 and Fred Sipman arrived as a veteran of defending champions the Los Angeles Aztecs. Additionally, Crowe retained Dave Landry, the second-choice goalkeeper on Seattle Sounders' debut club, and Roger Goldingay, an energetic forward who played in several games for the Sounders. Landry, a native of Saskatchewan, and Goldingay, who held dual American and British citizenship, were invited to the tryout based on their affiliation with the Sounders the year before. "It was much more limited than Seattle in 1974. It was only a couple of days so it was a mass tryout," remembers Goldingay. The manager running the tryout made no mistake about his intentions and his expected level of commitment. Goldingay says, "Vic Crowe was really an impressive coach. Very tough, hard-nosed kind of guy."

After steady rain in Thursday's tryout, Crowe welcomed sunshine at Catlin Gabel School for his decision-making day for the final three roster spots. More important to Crowe was the good news from England that the struggles with British and American immigration offices were finally resolved, save for two players, and that the arrival of the bulk of the squad would occur within forty-eight hours. The Timbers' manager oversaw a scrimmage at his tryout and invited fourteen players back for additional workouts over the coming weeks, postponing his decision on which three North Americans to sign. Landry and Goldingay were the favorites for two spots, though Crowe cited the ability to sign players to amateur contracts—meaning that if he did not want to, he did not have to specify which players would fill the required slots until the day of the first game.

Leo Crowther had been in England, missing the tryouts in his role as personnel deliveryman for Vic Crowe. Once the British government approved the group visa, Crowther could assemble the soon-to-be Timbers and accompany them to America. Portland's assistant coach remembers, "Days passed with no visa, despite transatlantic phone calls from Vic and the owners of the Timbers. Finally, the Friday before our Sunday flight, we were told that the visa was available at the U.S. consulate in Liverpool. As my own car was temporarily out of commission, I borrowed a red Ford Capri from John Gidman, a Villa player. I sped up from Birmingham, waited a few hours for paperwork to be completed and at last had that precious visa in my hand."

The tireless work of Crowther in England and Don Paul in the United States had finally secured the services of ten of the thirteen players of British origin yet to make their way to the United States. Only Graham Day, Tony Betts and Willie Anderson remained, with further immigration issues holding back the former two. Senator Bob Packwood was enlisted to work with the U.S. State Department to finalize the visas for Day and Betts. Anderson was still active as Cardiff City reached the Welsh Cup final against Wrexham.

The flight on Pan Am from London's Heathrow Airport to Seattle-Tacoma International Airport was an eleven-hour journey. On Sunday, April 27, 1975, ten members of the Portland Timbers and assistant coach Leo Crowther landed at Portland International Airport. Nearly every player had finished his season just the day before in a busy Saturday across England's Football League. Vic Crowe greeted the new Portland Timbers with a smile.

"Friday?" asked captain Brian Godfrey upon arrival in Portland. Tailed by his daughters, Rachel and Rebecca, and weary wife, Avril, the Timbers' skipper was unaware of the immediacy of Portland's first game when confronted by the local media. Quickly composing himself, suddenly aware of his role as captain, the thirty-four-year-old Godfrey responded, "Knowing Vic Crowe, and I've played under him before, he took his time selecting players. We just need a little time and a bit of luck." True to form, or perhaps simply to avoid the inevitable questions from his players, Crowe had never informed his players that their first test would come just six days after landing in Portland.

The new Timbers came to a city well prepared for their arrival. Despite having just three months to their name, the Portland Timbers' stockholders were at Portland's airport, eagerly awaiting their new employees. Mick and Linda Hoban were at the gate to welcome their new teammates, while a group of fans brought bouquets of roses for each of the six wives. "We were very quickly introduced to some people we'd never met who seemed willing to do anything they possibly could for us. Within the next few hours and days, they had taken us shopping, given us a car and settled us into the apartment. I thought I'd died and gone to heaven," muses Chris Dangerfield. The nineteen-year-old was on his first visit to America and was hoping to earn experience by playing over the summer. Dangerfield's teammate at Wolverhampton, Jimmy Kelly, was of a similar mind. "It's a chance to come visit America," Kelly announced at the airport. "It's a long way from home, but I thought I'd take a chance."

Crowe sent his new players to a local hotel to rest and prepare for the five-day experience of learning how to play together before their first game. Paul scheduled a public appearance for the team at Washington Square Mall at 11:00 a.m. on Monday, and Crowe had the first training session set for Tuesday at 9:30 a.m. The ten new British players retired to their hotel rooms with just five days between them and their first chance to impress their new hosts.

Monday morning came early for the British players, but it could not come soon enough for the North American players still waiting to learn their status with Vic Crowe. Having finally retrieved the majority of his players from the United Kingdom, Crowe focused on the American requirement long enough to sign three players from the previous week's tryouts. Dave Landry, the twenty-three-year-old goalkeeper; Roger Goldingay, the twenty-four-year-old forward; and Nick Nicolas, the twenty-three-year-old fullback, were added to the roster. Adding three North Americans fulfilled the league mandate[3] and completed the club's roster on the first day of "Portland Soccer Week," as declared by Mayor Neil Goldschmidt. That same day, the British contingent of the Timbers moved out of their hotel and into apartments at the Tall Firs complex in Beaverton. Crowe and Crowther were next door in the Timber Creek apartments. "Rather fitting for the Timbers, eh?" joked Crowe.

Nick Nicolas's 1975 NASL player card. Signed the day before Portland's second game, this card certified Nicolas as a formal member of both the Timbers and the NASL. *Courtesy of Nick Nicolas.*

Focusing on their domestic seasons until their departure, most of the British players in Portland knew very little about where they were headed. "I honestly thought that Portland was on the coast. As I came from the airport and up Highway 26, I thought the ocean must be on the other side of the hill," remembers Tony Betts. Willie Anderson, another late arrival, was not even sure of the club's nickname, telling a fellow passenger on his flight to the United States that he was coming to play soccer for the Portland Foresters. Chris Dangerfield was surprised at the differences between his home country and the United States, saying, "Everything seemed to be bigger and newer." Of course, not everything was different. "We came to a very rainy Portland. But we left rainy Birmingham, so it didn't make much difference."

The Timbers had the day off from training on Monday to get over their jet lag, but they hit the field for the first time on Tuesday morning. The fourteen players met at Civic Stadium for the first time, only to find a construction crew covering half of the playing surface. The reason for the shared space was the replacement of the stadium's six-year-old Tartan turf. With work only half done, the Timbers would have to accept a fifty-three-yard-wide field, barely the league minimum, for both training and early games. While spatial limitations hampered the first day's training, the bigger adjustment for the players was with the turf itself. "It's a bit awkward at first. Sometimes the ball stops dead and other times it shoots off. It's quite different for me," said Don Gardner. Brian Godfrey claimed, "It's a little rough out there right now, but our boys were picking it up toward the end of practice."

The experience was new not only for the players but also for the local media. Says Peter Withe, "I asked Chris and Jimmy to cross some balls in as a warm-up. I headed the first ball into the goal, and a cameraman nearly dropped his camera. They filmed me for about five minutes because they'd never seen someone head the ball. That's where I initially got the nickname 'Mad Header.'"

On April 30, the Timbers welcomed two more players. Tony Betts and Graham Day arrived from England, having overcome their troubles with British immigration. Despite his lack of time to prepare with the rest of the team, Day arrived in Portland expecting to be featured in the starting eleven in the first game.

Crowe kept a sunny disposition before the media, even with the challenges ahead. At an Oregon Sports Writers and Sportscasters luncheon, Crowe joked, "We have not had the ideal preparation that I'd like. In fact, I asked the players to stand when I introduced them today so they could meet each other."

Oregon Soccer, Inc., and the North American Soccer League

How ready was Portland for professional soccer in the spring of 1975? The *Oregonian* assumed very few Portlanders knew the rules of the game. Three consecutive Sunday *Oregonians* featured explanations of rules as dictated by Vic Crowe to their beat writer, John Polis. In the *Oregon Journal*, sports editor George Pasero conducted an interview where he was able to persuade Mick Hoban to admit that soccer was closely related to basketball.

Yet Portland had both a history of soccer and a growing contingent of youth and adult soccer leagues by early 1975. Association football was first played at Multnomah Field in October 1893 between Portland and Astoria teams. By 1908, the *Oregonian* featured a full-page story with accompanying "snapshots" of the opening game of the association football season between the Multnomah Amateur Athletic Club and a club called the Columbias. In the 1930s, it was common for the local German Sports Club to play matches against visiting sailors.

Throughout the history of soccer in Portland, ethnic teams carried on the tradition of their homelands, especially as the sport faded from the forefront of America's sporting consciousness. As American football and baseball emerged as the dominant sports, instances like a match between Scotsmen and Englishmen living in Portland in 1907 were eventually confined to smaller parks. Ethnic clubs like Sportclub Germania, The Clan and St. Patrick's each played a role in the continuation of soccer in Portland, though the real growth of local soccer came as children of immigrants stopped relying only on their ethnic clubs and began playing at school or with neighborhood club teams. Club games took place at Westmoreland, Columbia, Buckman and Montavilla Parks until 1960, when Delta Park opened. The ethnic teams continued to be important in the local scene, with Sportclub Germania even hosting West

Mick Hoban with *Oregon Journal* sports editor George Pasero. The two are holding *Terrific Timbers*, a publication sold after the season by the *Journal* to commemorate Portland's success in 1975. *Courtesy of Mick Hoban, personal collection.*

German professional club VfL Oldenburg at Franklin High School in the summer of 1971. But the amateur game was growing away from the ethnic clubs, particularly in the suburbs.

On October 26, 1974, John Gilbertson and Don Paul visited Centennial High School in Gresham. The reason for their attendance was to watch youth soccer games from the Mount Hood Junior Soccer Association, including the featured game between the Rockwood Rockets and Kent (Washington) Trappers. Gilbertson and Paul were not conducting a scouting trip, as the players in question were nine- and ten-year-olds. Three months later, after earning formal admission to the NASL, Paul told reporters, "We went to Delta Park, where soccer is being played every weekend, more than any other sport. We have about ten thousand people playing soccer in the immediate area. This is a springboard of something that's coming."

Clearly, soccer was an emerging sport in Portland, and a professional team could expect to host thousands of fans, if given a big enough stadium. The Seattle Sounders had played their initial season at a high school stadium holding thirteen thousand. Paul had grander visions for his Timbers and contacted city councilwoman Mildred Schwab. The ideal space for the Timbers was Civic Stadium, given its centrality in town, as well as its capacity of twenty-seven thousand. But as the name suggested, the stadium was owned by the city, and a rental agreement needed approval by the council before any club could play its games at the forty-nine-year-old stadium.

Civic Stadium was built in 1926 and opened to great fanfare by hosting the annual American football game between the University of Oregon and the University of Washington. The stadium was built by the Multnomah Amateur Athletic Club and was owned and operated as such until 1966. The club, in need of additional capital, sold the concrete stadium to the city for $2.1 million.

The second incarnation of a Portland franchise in the World Football League (WFL) was negotiating a deal for Civic Stadium when Paul and the Timbers formally met with Schwab. With pressure mounting, the city had leverage enough to command rental agreements far higher than the $750 per game charged the Portland Storm in 1974. On April 18, Mildred Schwab publically signed a contract with the Portland Timbers to lease Civic Stadium at a flat rate of $1,750 per game, plus expenses. The city ordinance had been passed on April 14 and posted by the city council on April 17 "authorizing an agreement between the city and Oregon Soccer, Inc., for use of Portland Civic Stadium for NASL games and related practices and

WATCH THE TIMBERS AT CIVIC STADIUM

Civic Stadium		Game Time 7:30	Civic Stadium		Game Time 7:30
Home	May 2	Friday	Seattle	Away	July 12	Saturday	At Boston
Home	May 7	Wednesday	Toronto	Away	July 16	Wednesday	At New York
Away	May 11	Sunday	At Denver	Away	July 19	Saturday	At St. Louis
Away	May 16	Friday	At Vancouver	Home	July 26	Saturday	Seattle
Home	May 27	Tuesday	Rochester	Home	July 29	Tuesday	San Jose
Home	May 30	Friday	Chicago	Away	August 2	Saturday	At Seattle
Home	June 7	Saturday	Vancouver	Away	August 9	Saturday	At Los Angeles
Away	June 14	Saturday	At San Jose				
Home	June 18	Wednesday	Dallas				
Home	June 21	Saturday	San Antonio				
Away	June 27	Friday	At Los Angeles				
Away	June 28	Saturday	At San Jose				
Home	July 3	Thursday	Vancouver				
Home	July 8	Tuesday	Los Angeles	LISTEN TO			
Away	July 11	Friday	At Hartford	TIMBERS SOCCER ON KOIN/970			

**For Ticket Information call
223-1173**

Interior of the 1975 pocket schedule showing dates, times and opponents for the Portland Timbers. *Courtesy of Nick Nicolas.*

activities of the team." The pact also allowed for the Timbers' selling of programs and soccer novelties at their games.

"Let me say simply that we're delighted to have you, and I'm sure the citizens of Portland are going to love soccer, love the Timbers and support the team in every way possible," declared a prescient Schwab at city hall. The 4–0 vote gave the Timbers a home and also engendered support for Schwab, the controversial but influential city councilwoman. In fact, Schwab wrote a check for her own season ticket during the announcement before trying to kick a ball to Mick Hoban, who was on hand for the occasion. While she did not miss entirely, Schwab did manage to blast the ball into a skylight above, sending reporters diving for cover.

With a home ground secured, the only issue left for the Timbers came in the form of the stadium's turf. On March 25, Schwab had orchestrated the replacement of the stadium's original Tartan turf covering, an artificial surface in place at Civic Stadium since 1969.[4] Six years of baseball, American football and rain had left the carpet in terrible condition and in desperate need of replacement. Schwab arranged for the 3M Company to completely overhaul the surface of the field with new Tartan turf at a cost of $225,000, with work set to begin on April 21. That timetable worked nicely for a potential football team and the Portland Mavericks, Portland's minor-league baseball team at the time. But the Timbers started training on the field just eight days after the start of the renovations and had their first game scheduled for May 2. Portland's first professional soccer team would simply have to live with the remnants of the nation's first multipurpose artificial turf until the work was complete.

2

Introductions in the Locker Room

It turned out that the woeful Tartan turf was but one of the problems for the Portland Timbers on the night of May 2, 1975. Rarely in history are events remembered in exactly the same way. Differing parties come to differing conclusions, particularly as time passes. Yet players and fans alike remember the inaugural Portland Timbers match at Civic Stadium in remarkably similar words. Mick Hoban: "We put all this effort into the first game, and we were out promoting the game, and on the day of the game it rained." Chris Dangerfield: "It rained, and there was a big pile of mud that used to be a baseball diamond right under the goal." Tony Betts: "The weather was unbelievable that summer, apart from the very first game." Leo Crowther: "The pitch was covered in pools of water. It was probably unplayable in England, but the referee gave us the go-ahead." Don Cox, an eighteen-year-old sitting in the bleachers on the west side of the stadium that night, recalls, "It was a rainy night, and we sat directly below where the roof ended, and the gutter was emptying down on us." Bernie Fagan,[5] then a Seattle Sounders' defender, remembers, "It was raining like hell, and they still had the bases in. They weren't covered, and they were muddy."

In front of 6,913 fans in the first professional soccer game in Oregon, the Portland Timbers lost 1–0 to the Seattle Sounders. Jimmy Gabriel slotted the game's only goal from the penalty spot in the twenty-ninth minute after a tripping foul was called on Barry Lynch. "We're so disappointed for the crowd because we wanted to do well for the people," said Ray Martin. Vic Crowe voiced similar sentiments after the game, saying, "We dominated

Tony Betts (14) dribbles into the mud of Civic Stadium's second base in the Timbers' season opener against the Seattle Sounders on May 2. Future Timbers defender Bernie Fagan (15) is trailing, while Brian Godfrey (6) and Mick Hoban (4) are in the background. *Courtesy Tony Betts, personal collection.*

them for ninety minutes. We played well, and the crowd was tremendous. My only disappointment is the result." Statistically, the Timbers did indeed dominate the Sounders, outshooting the visitors twenty-two to six, with fourteen corner kicks to Seattle's one. Portland even had a penalty shot of its own, taken by midfielder Barry Powell in the forty-eighth minute. Seattle's All-Star goalkeeper Barry Watling saved that shot, though the Timbers believed the Seattle keeper came off his line too soon.

Despite the frustration in controlling the tempo of a game significantly altered by weather, pitch size, shortened preparation time and the lack of a full squad, the Timbers players and coaches did see positives in their first game. Captain Brian Godfrey was optimistic, saying, "We couldn't have played much better under the conditions. I'll tell you one thing, if we play like that the rest of the year, we won't lose many more." After the game, Crowe focused on Kelly, the diminutive winger, noting, "Jimmy was exciting, and I think the fans like him. They'll come back just to watch him run." Even Walt Daggatt, Seattle's managing owner, had good things to say about the Timbers, declaring, "What a helluva team. Portland has great personnel. They'll raise hell in this league."

It was indeed Jimmy Kelly who first captured the imagination of soccer fans in Portland. While earning critical acclaim from fellow players and coaches, Kelly resonated most with the early supporters of the Timbers. Kurt Schubothe, then a twenty-year-old fan, remembers liking Kelly because "he was very quick on his feet and made amazing runs." Kelly was so small, standing just five-foot-six, that it was difficult for his teammates to even see him from across the field. "The field crowned in the middle and took a dip on the other side. So if you were sitting on the bench, you could only see the top of Jimmy's head!" says Chris Dangerfield. The *Oregon Journal* devoted an entire column to the initial cult status of Jimmy Kelly the day before the Timbers' second game. "Kelly dazzled both the fans and the Seattle defenders with lightning-quick footwork as he dribbled the ball with contorted moves down the sidelines and into the corners before usually getting off a centering pass or a corner shot. Once, he faked two Sounders into each other," raved the *Journal's* John Nolen. Though fewer than seven thousand witnessed Kelly's first game in Portland, the winger picked up the nickname "Magic Feet" and was an acknowledged hit with the female portion of the audience.

Despite the loss, fans of all ages were enthralled by the quickness of Jimmy Kelly, the grit and poise of Brian Godfrey and Ray Martin, the speed of Don Gardner and the powerful front man Peter Withe. Seventy-year-old David Kinnear said after the first game, "Ever since I came here from Scotland in the mid-1920s, I've dreamed of having this kind of soccer here. I wouldn't have missed tonight for anything."

THE TEAM'S FIRST GAME WAS hardly the only responsibility of the Timbers players in the early days of the season. Despite dominating the game in nearly every way, the players were still very much getting used to their new lives in the United States. Part of that acclimatization came in the form of sponsor families. Prior to their arrival, each player was assigned to a particular family in the community, many of whom were investors in OSI. Mick Hoban was placed with John Gilbertson's family; Tommy McLaren was given local soccer referee Bernie Rilatt's family; Willie Anderson, though not yet arrived in Portland, was given to Clarence Wicks and family; Peter Withe, to OSI treasurer Don Harper; Graham Brown, to Don Pollock; and so on. Each family was responsible for helping the Timbers furnish their apartments and purchase linens, dishes and pots and pans. Directions to grocery stores, restaurants, bars and vacation locales were supplied, and several cars were leased to the team to be used collectively. "It was a successful way to have people settle pretty quickly," says Linda Hoban, who had experienced transition in two previous NASL cities.

Single players were also challenged in adjusting, as they were younger and without the benefit of other family members on which to rely. "The guys who were married, and their wives, made sure we were taken care of

Donald Gardner, Jimmy Kelly and Chris Dangerfield in the locker room. With Barry Powell, the four players were on loan from Wolverhampton Wanderers and were popularly known as the "Timber Wolves." *Courtesy Chris Dangerfield, personal collection.*

in the early days. As did the sponsor families. They were generous not only with their time, but also with their homes and families," remembers Chris Dangerfield, one of the so-called "Timber Wolves." This group consisted of four single youngsters from Wolverhampton Wanderers: Dangerfield, nineteen; Don Gardner, nineteen; Jimmy Kelly, twenty-one; and Barry Powell, twenty-one.

Due to the four-month contracts signed by every player, no long-term living arrangements were necessary. So OSI made a deal with an apartment complex in Beaverton and had each player live within several units of one another. Tall Firs was the name of the complex, advertising itself as having "15 acres of the most exciting happening in the Northwest…where quality blends with gracious living." Leo Crowther offers a more realistic version of the simple housing, saying, "The apartments were two-story buildings and painted brown." Crowther and Crowe lived next door in the Timber Creek apartments on Northwest Barnes Road.

Eight of the players had families, and seven had children. The wives and families were given specific attention by their respective sponsor families, while Jan Gilbertson was an ever-present guide. Though the wives "spent the first game explaining soccer to American men," according to a group interview in the Sunday *Oregonian*, the challenges involved in moving to a foreign country for just four months were myriad. From sending mail back home to acquiring the necessary tools for cleaning, cooking and enjoying their down time, the British wives needed adjustment time just as much as their husbands. "We were out in Beaverton, and they couldn't get around as easily because we had all the cars," explains Tony Betts.

Loneliness and isolation were not always the case, though, according to Mick Hoban. "When we left practice, we all went back to the same apartment complex and were very communal. We constantly saw our teammates throughout the week, and we knew their spouses and their kids. It really was more of a family feel." Despite the difficulties inherent in relocating to a new country, Linda Hoban explains, "for the families it was almost like an extended vacation."

Apart from day-to-day life and family adjustments, the players were also immediately expected to adjust to their new lives as the Portland Timbers.

The Tall Firs apartment complex on Northwest Barnes Road in Beaverton. The complex was home to all seventeen players and their families. *Courtesy of Chris Dangerfield, personal collection.*

Mostly that meant training sessions with the incredibly competitive Vic Crowe. Training was the area where Crowe's traditional roots bled through more than any other setting. "Run. Kick. Run," was the reality of the physically challenging workouts on the Tartan turf, according to Tony Betts. The turf wore on the knees of the players used to playing on true grass back in England. "When it rained, the pitch was a mess, and when it was hot, it was hard as concrete. It was the worst I ever played on," Betts remembers. With Crowe in charge and Crowther assisting, the Timbers engaged in running exercises and short, small-sided games at every training session. "Vic was specific in his expectations for players," says Dave Landry. "He was very analytical. It was clear that coaching was his profession."

After fitness training was complete, the goalkeepers and outfield players split. Landry and Graham Brown worked together apart from the rest of the team, with Brown taking a teaching role. "I learned more about goalkeeping from Graham Brown than anyone else," Landry says of the one-on-one tutelage. Says Brown, "Dave had a great work ethic and was keen to improve his knowledge of the game." The pairing of goalkeepers was a healthy one and kept both sharp throughout the season.

Both the constant running and the small-sided games were integral parts of the experience of the 1975 Portland Timbers. Crowe's philosophy on winning came from an expectation of impeccable physical fitness. "He wanted to make sure that his team was extremely well prepared and fit. Vic took it very seriously. The trainings were always competitive, and they were hard," recalls Chris Dangerfield. The games in training brought out the best in players and even in the manager himself. "We would play five-a-sides, and Crowe's team would never leave the field until he had won. Vic was nasty on the field," says Hoban. Roger Goldingay remembers the practice games being even more focused than real games, adding, "I don't think we ever played more than two-touch in practice. Half the practice was one-touch."

The antidote to Crowe's toughness was Leo Crowther. The fifty-two-year-old assistant coach had his own particular skill set, not necessarily based in assertiveness and intensity. Crowther had been hired by Crowe to be his youth and reserve team coach at Aston Villa in 1970 and won the FA Youth Cup at Villa in 1972, with Tony Betts among the star players. Mick Hoban had also played under Crowther in the Villa reserve team prior to moving to America. Unlike many involved in English football at the time, Crowther did not fit the mold of hard-living, rough, working-class lads. "He was an educated man, so he stuck out in professional football because he was well read and well spoken. He was like a teacher," says Hoban. Crowther was a very important calming force in training sessions, taking advantage of the role of "good guy" to Crowe's "bad guy," particularly with those players not as familiar with Vic's style. Crowther would follow up after Crowe, assuring players that they were not being singled out and giving encouragement. Importantly, Crowe trusted his assistant, respected Crowther's style and did not encroach on it.

Apart from training and running, the Timbers players engaged in a constant series of public appearances on behalf of the club and, in a larger sense, the game of soccer. Speaking engagements at the YMCA, schools and community centers, as well as clinics and demonstrations, were significant parts of the players' lives after their morning practices. Leo Crowther, whose second role was community development officer, led a ten-week coaching course at Portland Community College and created a fourteen-page pamphlet with drills to be used in youth soccer practices. Crowther reached the public through local television and as the color commentary for KOIN radio's broadcasts of Timbers games, in addition to regular educational sessions in and around the city. Bringing the game to the community was a promise of Vic Crowe's after being named head coach in Portland. "I'm going to bring players over here who can not only play but have a relationship off the field," he said. "We want players who will work with youngsters. It's important to get among the community and help develop soccer in the Portland area."

Mick Hoban in a promotional photo shoot at Civic Stadium. The Timbers tried to involve themselves in the community at every opportunity, particularly in 1975, hoping to attract fans in Portland. *Courtesy of Mick Hoban, personal collection.*

Yet all the positives surrounding the Timbers were in contrast to the result of the first fixture. With a loss and no goals to show for their first outing, the Timbers were optimistic but frustrated. The biggest point of contention was the pitch itself and the daily struggle to find adequate shoes. "They hadn't yet designed a soccer shoe for artificial turf. There were football and baseball shoes, but we couldn't use those. So we were wearing Adidas trainers, green with yellow stripes," Dangerfield remembers. With molded shoes, indoor shoes and cleated shoes all familiar to the England-based players, footwear was not in short supply on the plane across the Atlantic. But shoes that could be worn on the Tartan turf at Civic Stadium were much harder to come by. OSI made a deal with Oregon Athletic Equipment, Inc., a sporting goods store on Northeast Sandy Boulevard, to allow the Timbers players to pick up new pairs of the stylish Adidas trainers by simply signing for them. Several players recall a liberal attitude throughout the team in regards to the number of pairs of shoes acquired from the store during the season. Still, in the first game of the year, the players were adjusting not only to the artificial turf and the new shoes but also to the pouring rain and the inability to keep their footing. One of the low points in the opening match was Barry Powell's circus-like splash, bringing even the home support to audible laughter. Given the shot disparity against Seattle, it was clear that the Portland players could bring the ball off the turf and toward an opposing goalkeeper in their shoes. The question was whether or not the Timbers could use those shoes to find the back of the net.

Just five days after their initial foray into the NASL, the Timbers hosted Toronto Metros-Croatia at Civic Stadium. The Timbers needed a win, or at least a goal, while Toronto was also off to a poor start. Toronto, with its hyphenated name, was a club based on a merger of the Toronto Metros of the NASL and Toronto Croatia, a successful ethnic club in the Canadian National Soccer League. Though the NASL was more widely known in the United States, the powerhouse ethnic clubs, particularly in Toronto, were probably better than the NASL champions in the early years of the league.

The Timbers trotted out a lineup similar to their opening game, featuring Peter Withe up top with Jimmy Kelly and Donald Gardner on the wings. Barry Powell, Tommy McLaren and Brian Godfrey filled the midfield, while Mick Hoban, Ray Martin, Barry Lynch and Graham Day defended in front of goalkeeper Graham Brown. Civic Stadium's pitch was still just fifty-three yards wide, squeezing Vic Crowe's formation into a narrow line and forcing more direct play.

In the thirty-third minute, Withe sent a powerful header off the goalpost. Instead of responding with frustration, the Timbers immediately blasted another shot at Toronto keeper Željko Bilecki. The Croatian-born Canadian deflected Jimmy Kelly's shot into the air, leaving Withe an open net for another headed attempt. This time the header was true, giving Portland its first-ever goal. Meanwhile, the Timbers' defense played as well as they had against Seattle, forcing Graham Brown into only three saves. The ambition of attack dropped off significantly after Withe's goal, though Portland was able to hold off Toronto to earn a 1–0 victory. Crowe was not pleased with the overall effort, despite the win, saying, "Unfortunately we quit playing, especially in the second half. We seemed to fear losing what we had, and we restricted ourselves and lost momentum." Captain Brian Godfrey agreed, adding, "We're not too happy with our second half. But I think we were a bit desperate for a win."

The win over Toronto was the last home game for the Timbers for three weeks as work was scheduled to conclude the replacement of Civic Stadium's Tartan turf surface. The new carpet's installation promised to give Portland not only a better surface but also a widening of the pitch. Though Crowe was effectively playing with two wingers on the fifty-three-yard-wide pitch, the lack of width prevented both outside forwards from effectively stretching their opponents' defense. Jimmy Kelly was a true winger, but Crowe's right-sided players in the first two matches were Donald Gardner and Tony Betts, both of whom were more traditional forwards. Though Withe was clearly a target as the center forward, his service mostly came from Kelly on the left side. Portland's inability to double the attack by having another wide player on the right threatened to reduce its scoring opportunities. Barry Powell and Tommy McLaren were pushing into attack in the central midfield, and either Gardner or Betts were drifting toward the center. Withe could see the problem developing in front of him as he played with his back to the goal in the traditional English center forward style. "Toronto put more men at midfield and crowded us, and on the smaller field that hurt us." Portland was, of course, also missing a vital piece of the team selected by Crowe earlier in the spring. Cardiff City winger Willie Anderson had yet to arrive, as his Bluebirds were playing in the Welsh Cup final against Wrexham. Anderson's inclusion on a wider pitch would give the Timbers their dual-attacking wingers and keep the team from getting mired in the midfield.

Portland's first away game of the season came four days later against Denver Dynamos in suburban Lakewood, Colorado. While the Dynamos often played their home games at cavernous Mile High Stadium near downtown Denver, the game against the Timbers was seven miles to the west at the ten-thousand-seat Jefferson County Stadium. As a high school football field, Jeffco was only able to accommodate a fifty-eight-yard-wide pitch. The game was not a good one for the Timbers. Mike Flater[6] scored in the eleventh minute for the home side, immediately putting Portland in the position of needing to score rather than allowing goal-scoring opportunities to develop. The Timbers were given a man-advantage when Denver's Peter Short punched Tommy McLaren in the face, splitting his lip in the twenty-fifth minute. That punch earned Short a red card and gave Portland a chance to level terms. Peter Withe finally got the Timbers on the score line with another rebounded goal, this time from a Graham Day shot that was saved by Denver keeper Richard Blackmore. Withe's second goal of the season was almost immediately followed up by a goal from Barry Powell, but the referee waved it off, judging Powell to have scored from an offside position.

After Powell's goal was disallowed, Denver reestablished control of the game and pilloried Portland's defense over the final fifteen minutes. Shaka Ngcobo, a South African player who assisted on Flater's opener for the Dynamos, scored the second goal for the home side at seventy-four minutes. Five minutes later, Ace Ntsoelengoe, a star on loan from Kaiser Chiefs, scored for Denver, putting the game out of reach. Late in the game, Graham Day was given a red card of his own, adding further disappointment for the well-beaten Timbers. Tony Betts did appear to pull one back for Portland in the game's dying moments, but he too was called offside. Crowe was so upset with the performance that he put his team back to work in a difficult two-hour training session at Catlin Gabel School less than twenty hours after the humiliating defeat. "We're disappointed because we know we can do better. We gave up three bad goals," Crowe lamented. A narrow pitch, an inability to create chances for Withe and lapses in defense again undid the Timbers. "We need goals. That's the simple ingredient. You can't win without them," Crowe added. Worryingly for Crowe and Portland, their next opponents were the Vancouver Whitecaps, the league's top team.

Willie Anderson and the 4-3-3

Willie Anderson was the seventeenth and final member of the Portland Timbers. Anderson's flight to the United States came on May 14, twelve days after the Timbers' first game. While Crowe would have certainly preferred to have had the twenty-eight-year-old veteran of Manchester United, Aston Villa and, most recently, Cardiff City prior to the start of the season, the timing of Anderson's arrival in Portland could not have been better. With central defender Graham Day set to miss the game in Vancouver due to his red card at Denver, Crowe was shuffling his lineup anyway. Adding Anderson on the right wing, opposite Jimmy Kelly, gave Crowe flexibility to move midfielders without affecting his goal-scoring threats of Withe, Kelly and Powell. Additionally, Vancouver's Empire Stadium featured a sixty-eight-yard-wide pitch, giving Portland's wingers room to truly take advantage of their unique skills.

Anderson arrived in Portland but did not train with the team before flying north for the Vancouver game. The Liverpudlian winger used his Thursday to move his family into the apartment complex where the rest of his teammates lived.

While the rest of the British-based Timbers were growing used to the unique rules and styles of the NASL, Anderson lagged behind. Though he spent five weeks with Aston Villa playing in the NASL's 1969 season,[7] Anderson was unaware of some of the particulars of the American version of the game. Upon arriving in the dressing room in Vancouver, Anderson remembers, "I got my shirt, it's got my name on it and it's got the number twelve. Well in England, that means you're on the bench because the first eleven play. So I was pissed off. And everyone just started laughing; they said, 'No, you keep that for the whole season.'"

With his kit and position in the team figured out, Anderson joined his new teammates on the pitch against the undefeated Vancouver Whitecaps. Instead of confusion ensuing with a new player and new positions for several others, the Timbers completely dominated the Canadian side. Barry Powell ripped a stunning forty-yard goal in the tenth minute after a back-heel from Anderson. Portland scored again five minutes later when Tony Betts nodded in a headed pass from Peter Withe. Withe had two shots rattle Vancouver keeper Peter Greco's crossbar in the second half and a goal called back for offside. Even defender Barry Lynch got in on the offensive blitz, scoring a goal that was also called back for offside. But it was Anderson who made all the difference. According to Crowe, "Willie played all the way at forward even though he arrived from England just two days ago. It's unbelievable the way he played on Tartan turf for the first time in his life. It was like he had played on it all along."

Portland's offensive explosion gained all the headlines, and with good reason. Only two goals in the first three games gave way to two more against the league's top team. Yet the most interesting facet of the match was not necessarily the action on the pitch but the formation and style employed by Crowe and the Timbers. With Day missing the game in central defense, Crowe elected to move captain Brian Godfrey from his holding midfielder[8] role back into defense instead of adding a fourth defender. Crowe took his remaining three defenders, Mick Hoban, Barry Lynch and Ray Martin, out of a zonal-marking scheme and into strict man marking against the high-flying Whitecaps. Hoban marked Vancouver's Brian Mitchell, while Martin was given the task of shutting down top scorer Sergio Zanatta. That man-to-man defending gave Godfrey the flexibility to aid in defense as a sweeper but also to emerge from defense and initiate attack from his extremely deep-lying position. "I was to tie the loose ends and pick up any man who got through," the Timbers' skipper explained.

Having Withe at center with Kelly and Anderson on his wings, Crowe still had three open midfield positions now that Godfrey was a fourth defender. Tony Betts was given his first start as a third midfielder, joining McLaren and Powell. McLaren dropped deeper, allowing for the much more offensively minded Powell and Betts to take off in support of the three forwards. Betts rewarded Crowe's decision by scoring the Timbers' second goal against Vancouver, while the inclusion of Anderson on the right wing gave Portland a balanced attack in the final third. Said Crowe immediately after the upset victory, "It was a good all-around performance by everyone, but the important thing was our discipline and concentration, which we didn't have last Sunday at Denver."

"Two out-and-out wingers would have been rare to nonexistent in England in 1975 but common in the Netherlands or West Germany; 4-3-3 with a sweeper is the classic Total Football formation. Sweepers did exist in England—Dave Mackay was a sweeper under Brian Clough at Derby County—but were uncommon," says tactics expert Jonathan Wilson. Crowe's choice of running a sweeper alongside two pure wingers was rare in the largely Anglo-centric NASL. Crowe was clearly not, however, trying to implement Total Football in Portland, as the Timbers' lineup was not fluid. Nor was the formation new to Crowe, as he had perfected the style with his Third Division champion Aston Villa side in 1971–72, with Anderson and Ray Graydon as wingers.[9]

A 2-2 record saw the Timbers head back to Portland with renewed energy and hope for the future. Adding Anderson gave Portland an entirely new dimension, as his confidence and control—not to mention his pinpoint crosses—brought an ease of play. Playing four games in two weeks had also tired the team, and an eleven-day break due to construction at Civic Stadium was well earned. During the off week, Brian Godfrey was honored as a member of the NASL's weekly all-star team as a defender after playing sweeper in Vancouver. The time off from games also allowed Crowe to begin a television show on KATU with Dick Carr, the station's sports director, discussing the team, showing highlights and interviewing fans. Even the players got a chance to expand their horizons during the break. Tony Betts and Graham Day were celebrity guests of the Oregon Open Darts Championship at Oaks Park. The Timbers duo squared off against tournament players and local media in a celebrity game to open the sixth annual tournament. Portland had a three-game home stand ahead, with the Rochester Lancers, the Chicago Sting and Vancouver all visiting Civic Stadium in a ten-day period bridging late May and early June. The players and coaches took advantage of their time to rest by relaxing poolside at their apartment complex. The Timbers would not have another stretch of more than seven days off the rest of the season.

By the time the Rochester Lancers arrived in Portland for their match on May 27, the Timbers were well rested and ready to prevent their season from continuing in an up-and-down manner. Portland debuted its new pitch, now seventy-five yards wide, in the hopes that the extra width and the addition of

The pool at the Tall Firs apartment complex was the site of countless hours of enjoyment for the players and their children. *Courtesy of Chris Dangerfield, personal collection.*

Willie Anderson would allow for a second consecutive win and a modicum of stability early in the season.

Instead of smoothly sweeping past Rochester, the Timbers encountered an extremely physical match. The Lancers did not let the additional width bother them, even after going a man down on the half hour. Brian Godfrey gave Portland the lead after twenty-five minutes on a wonderful free kick after Rochester's Józef Janduda picked up a yellow card for an overly aggressive challenge. Godfrey replied with an arcing free kick over the wall, beating Ardo Perri to the top right corner. Just four minutes later, the Lancers were reduced to ten men when Ghanaian international defender George Lamptey earned a straight red card for his assault on Tony Betts. The two nearly came to blows, and Lamptey was sent off for his troubles. While Lamptey and Betts considered duking it out on the pitch, Vic Crowe and Frank Odoi, another Ghanaian international, fought on the touchline.

Though the game settled slightly after the mayhem of the middle of the first half, Rochester continued to play very physically. The Timbers were unhappy when ten-man Rochester equalized in the thirty-sixth minute on a Tommy Ord header. Portland went back ahead just two minutes after half time when Peter Withe scored one of his patented headed goals from a Jimmy Kelly cross, seemingly putting the Timbers back in control of the game. But Ed Jijon got a goal in the eighty-seventh minute to level the score again for Rochester. The Ecuadorian forward crashed into Timbers' keeper Graham Brown, keeping with the game's propensity for collisions, before knocking the ball into the net for the late equalizer.

With the score level after ninety minutes, the two sides entered overtime—Portland's first such endeavor of the season. Luckily for the 6,918 fans in attendance, the Timbers had Willie Anderson. After nearly seven minutes had passed in the golden-goal overtime period, Kelly whipped a cross into the box toward Withe. The Timbers' center forward got his head on the ball, but not cleanly enough to do any more than send it up into the air, drifting to the right side of the goal. Anderson met the ball on the volley as it dropped back toward the brand-new Tartan turf, smacking a shot past Perri and into Timbers' lore. "It sure took a long time to come down. I thought someone would come out and block it, so I just whacked it," Anderson modestly recalled in the dressing room.

The goal was the first of the season for the winger in only his second game with the club. After the combination of Kelly, Withe and Anderson resulted in the match-winner in overtime, it was clear that Crowe's vision for his team was complete. Strength up the middle with speed and skill on the wings gave Portland a unique style, one perfectly suited for the new and improved Civic Stadium. Two further home games could give Portland an opportunity to gain ground in the very difficult Western Division.

Chicago's team, named after the movie *The Sting*, had played the Israeli national team to a 2–2 draw earlier in the week and was coached by Bill Foulkes, a former teammate of Willie Anderson at Manchester United. The Timbers were set to play again without a starting defender, as Mick Hoban had injured his thigh against Rochester and was deemed unfit for the Chicago match on the weekend. Crowe planned to move Brian Godfrey back to sweeper, the role he had executed so well against Vancouver when

Graham Day was absent due to red card suspension. That switch meant another start for Tony Betts alongside Barry Powell and Tommy McLaren in the midfield. Portland also adjusted its pitch size again, this time reducing the width by a few yards, setting the field at 110 yards long and 72 yards wide for the remainder of the season.

As the Timbers and Sting prepared to meet on Friday night, news spread of a car accident in Eugene, Oregon, in the early hours of Friday morning. Track star Steve Prefontaine, the greatest hero in Oregon sports, had died. The *Oregon Journal*, Portland's afternoon newspaper, reported Prefontaine's passing in its Friday, May 30 edition, pushing the Timbers into the category of everything else. Portland hosted Chicago that night as Oregonians mourned.

The key for the Timbers against Chicago was defending Gordon Hill, the Sting's extraordinary winger. Portland's British contingent was well aware of Hill's exploits at Millwall. The youngster scored twenty-two goals in his two seasons at the London club and expected to make a big-money move upon his return from a summer in the NASL. Crowe decided to man mark Hill, putting Ray Martin on the twenty-one-year-old left winger, leaving Day, Barry Lynch and Godfrey, as sweeper, to corral the rest of the Chicago attack.

Crowe was again proven to be as smart as he was hard, as Portland easily defeated Chicago 2–0 for its third consecutive win. Martin kept Hill in check, only allowing him two shots over the ninety minutes at Civic Stadium. Day excelled in his role as sole central defender, and goalkeeper Graham Brown was forced to make just two saves on the night. In fact, Brown never even took off his tracksuit. Portland's stifling defense may have earned Brown his third clean sheet of the young season, but the offensive display was just as impressive. Willie Anderson scored his second goal of the season on what Foulkes called an impossible shot in the fortieth minute. Foulkes was quite impressed with Anderson's goal, saying, "I played with Willie in 1965 when he was seventeen, and he didn't score like that then!"

Anderson's goal came against Chicago defender John Webb. Anderson faked with a hard head and shoulder dip to the left, leaving Webb lunging and freeing up just enough space to rifle a shot from an acute angle. The angle was so sharp that Sting keeper Mervyn Cawston did not consider a shot as an option until the ball was past him and into the net for the Timbers' opener. Portland doubled its lead when Peter Withe chipped Cawston in the forty-seventh minute. Barry Powell's cross brought Cawston off his line, and Withe played the ball from a high bounce, neatly poking over the keeper for a 2–0 lead. Chicago responded with a Hill goal just four minutes later, but it was waved off for a mysterious offside call. Foulkes was unhappy with the result in terms of the referee's decision but gave credit to the Timbers for punishing his side when given the chance, saying, "I don't want to take anything away from Portland. They were very aggressive, very tenacious in every way. They very much deserved to win." The impressive victory was witnessed by 9,526 fans at Civic Stadium, the largest crowd of the season.

Portland was indeed earning a reputation as a hard team. With determined veterans mixed with ambitious youngsters, the Timbers had a strong nucleus. "I'm very pleased with the attitude of the players, and not just the players who are playing. This is something we have developed in a very short time. It's a togetherness that usually takes much longer for a team to develop," raved Crowe. Perhaps Crowe was so fond of his team, not just because he had personally selected each and every one of them to fit his mold, but also because the team was actually taking on his personality. "He was very intense, and he was very fierce. He loved to intimidate other teams. He would stand on the sideline, and he would yell at the opposing players," Nick Nicolas recalls. Crowe's tenacity from the touchline was spilling onto the field, making even the more mild-mannered players more intense. Nicolas adds, "Barry Lynch was not as hard a player, but for a guy that didn't look mean at all, he became very tough."

A 4-2 record and three-game winning streak saw the Timbers conclude their first month. With a complete team and relatively few injuries, Portland was established as a serious team, despite its last place position in the West Division. Portland finally found its scoring touch, rebounding from just two goals over its first three games to add seven more over the next three with goals coming from five different players. With more goals scored and the team winning, attendance was also creeping upward. The 9,526 on hand for the Chicago game showed the club's front office the realistic possibility of averaging 10,000 per game for the season. Having presumed that an average of roughly 6,500 per game would keep investors from losing money, Portland was on the path of survival. The early 1970s were a difficult time for the NASL as clubs frequently folded or moved to new cities. The Timbers appeared to be part of the success story on the West Coast, and the crowds responded accordingly. With a week off to prepare for another clash with Vancouver, the Timbers could look back on their first month as a success.

A week off for the Timbers meant time to relax. After temperatures had hovered mostly in the sixties throughout May, the beginning of June saw eighties and nineties for the first time that season. Warmer temperatures, afternoons off after training and a communal swimming pool at the Tall Firs complex brought the summer in the States to full reality. Willie Anderson best describes the enjoyment and relaxation: "We were finished at noon, so we'd go back to the apartment complex and sit around the pool having a beer with the wives and kids. It was just like being on holiday. Blitz, the major brewery, was a sponsor, and they used to give us free beer. So it was just dreamland." In fact, Blitz beer was a significant part of the Timbers' daily life, particularly after the team realized the connection between the brewery and the club. "Our favorite place was the Blitz brewery because it was right across the street from the stadium. Not sure what sponsorship they gave us except free beer every Friday afternoon. We knew one of the beer makers, Earl, and he would let us into the tasting room," remembers Tony Betts.

A week off was not the only time the Timbers enjoyed a few beers, though. As was common in British football at the time, as well as in sports like baseball, players had beer available in the dressing room following their games. "If we won games, the first thing we'd have was a bottle of beer. Most everybody would have a couple pops before they headed to the Hilton or the Benson. But nobody looked upon that as anything but normal," says Mick Hoban.

While beer was quite common in professional sports, post-game parties with fans certainly were not. The Trail Blazers basketball team was well known in town, but they were not as approachable as the affable Timbers, partly due to physical size and partly because of access. After each home game, the Timbers hosted a party, open to the public, at either the Benson Hotel or the downtown Hilton Hotel. The purpose of the parties was to engage the public and introduce the players to Americans and American culture. Making the Timbers available and accessible to any fan fostered a sense of community. The parties were a hit as supporters could buy their favorite players a beer, chat with them and extend the social event that Timbers' games were becoming long into the night. "We'd have five thousand people show up at the hotel reception. We couldn't even get upstairs into the ballroom where it was held because there were so many people," recalls Roger Goldingay.

Of course, Vic Crowe always kept watch over his players, even at the entirely social post-game parties. "If he could see the lads were having a beer or two, we were training the next day and were running again to make sure we were ready for the next game," Chris Dangerfield says. Despite Crowe's next-day training sessions, the players enjoyed their ability to mix with the community and get to know their supporters.

As temperatures cooled back into the sixties by the end of the week off and the Timbers began preparing in earnest for the rematch with the Vancouver Whitecaps, two injuries emerged. Through the first month of the season, Portland's players had kept mostly free of injury. But as the summer months arrived, niggling bumps and bruises started to accumulate and result in longer-term injuries. Mick Hoban was set to miss his second match with a thigh bruise, pushing Brian Godfrey back into a defensive role and opening up his midfield position to Tony Betts. Godfrey himself was the subject of a scare when he was bitten on the

Ray Martin at a post-game party in downtown Portland. These parties were a chance for fans to meet their favorite players and mingle with professional athletes. *Courtesy of Stella Terry, personal collection.*

heel by a neighbor's dog at the apartment complex. A tetanus shot was administered and his movements monitored by trainer Ron Culp, but Godfrey was ultimately declared fit enough to resume his role as captain. Still, the prospect of losing both the captain and a defender simultaneously forced Vic Crowe to consider using some of his substitute players. Situational resting of starters would be a necessity in the coming weeks. In the meantime, Vancouver would be short captain Les Wilson and scoring threat Sergio Zanatta due to injuries of their own.

Brian Godfrey's heel may have been bitten earlier in the week, but his foot was true when it mattered most. The Timbers' captain blasted a thirty-five-yard free kick into the net in overtime, lifting Portland to an important 3–2 win at home over the Whitecaps. The stunning goal shocked the Whitecaps and elated the club-record 11,335 fans in attendance.

"It was a goal fitting of a captain," beamed Vic Crowe. Not only did the victory keep Portland's winning streak alive, now at a healthy four games, but Godfrey's blast also provided the Timbers with the inaugural Columbia Cup. The trophy was devised as a derby competition between the two clubs in the style of rival clubs in England. By winning the first two games of the three-game series in 1975, the Timbers were guaranteed to win the cup—the first trophy in club history. Though their status as Columbia Cup champion was confirmed, the awarding of the trophy would have to wait until the third match later in the summer.

The match was no pushover for the Timbers, though, as Crowe referred to the contest as the most difficult game of the season. Twice coming from a goal down against its Northwest rivals, Portland relied on its trademark headers to keep the winning streak alive. The Timbers' first goal came from an unlikely source as Graham Day headed in from a yard out to equalize for Portland just moments after half time. An impassioned speech by Crowe during the interval inspired the Timbers, and a heading combination saw the leveler from the lanky defender. Tony Betts headed into the middle of the box toward Peter Withe, who in turn flicked on to Day to nod into the net for his first goal of the season. Day was the Timbers' one defender who both enjoyed and excelled at pushing forward into attack. Though Crowe limited his movements, Day could take advantage of his height in set pieces and through the odd marauding break toward goal.

The Whitecaps replied with a great goal, a twenty-five-yard blast from Glen Johnson, in the seventy-third minute. Yet Portland fired back just six minutes later with a fine goal from Betts. Willie Anderson lifted a chip into the box, allowing Betts to run onto it and head past Greg Weber for the Timbers' second equalizer. The seventy-ninth-minute goal was enough to bring the game to overtime, Portland's second such encounter of the young season. As had been the case against Rochester eleven days earlier, Portland got the game-winning goal before penalties and won 3–2.

Yet a four-game winning streak and a place among the top teams in the league could not prepare the Timbers for their first experience in San Jose. A week after their come-from-behind victory against Vancouver, Portland made the first of three appearances in Spartan Stadium, home of the Earthquakes. Having led the league in attendance in their inaugural year of 1974, the Earthquakes were vying again with Seattle as the league's most-watched club. They featured a roster heavy with Yugoslavian players, including Ilija Mitić, the NASL's all-time leading scorer. Mitić was traded to San Jose after just three games of the 1975 season. Though he was new to San Jose, the Yugoslavian star was a key for the Earthquakes.

The Bay Area, and San Jose in particular, had a long history of soccer in the semiprofessional and professional ranks, as well as in club teams and collegiate soccer.[10] The Timbers had a product of the San Jose soccer scene in defender Nick Nicolas. Nicolas had played with Earthquakes' forward

Archie Roboostoff[11] in high school, the latter of whom had a significant impact on the initial meeting between the Timbers and Earthquakes.

What the Timbers did not know ahead of their trip south was how rowdy the supporters of the Earthquakes were and what a loose hold the club's management had on the playing conditions at Spartan Stadium. San Jose employed a high school teacher named George Henderson to rile up the Earthquakes' supporters before, during and after matches. Better known as Krazy George, the longhaired, drum-banging madman ran around the stadium and led chanting San Jose fans.

Before a supercharged, sell-out crowd of 17,889, Mitić opened scoring after seventeen minutes with Dan Counce assisting. Tempers flared early and often between the clubs, leading to a second half of unmatched ferocity. By the end of the game, seventy-one fouls had been called, and three players were given red cards. The fighting began ten minutes after half time when the Timbers' Graham Day and the Earthquakes' Derek Craig traded blows. Both were immediately sent off and continued fighting into the tunnel.

Before the worst of the mêlées occurred, Portland drew even with a clever goal by Tony Betts. Tommy McLaren chipped a pass forward, giving Betts the opportunity to take a shot with his left foot, a shot he buried in the upper-right corner of Mike Ivanow's goal. The equalizer came in the sixty-fifth minute, leaving both sides, each on ten men, plenty of time to find a winner.

Five minutes later, the game got completely out of hand when thirty-seven-year-old player-coach Gabbo Gavrić earned a straight red for roughing. Fouls, fights and pitch invasions ensued. Portland's Powell was whistled for a foul in the seventy-fifth minute for kicking Boris Bandov in the ribs. The referee's calling of the foul was not quick enough for San Jose assistant coach Ivan Toplak. Running across the field to challenge the referee, Toplak's eruption led to confusion in the stadium. While players from both sides stood by waiting to see the referee's reaction, a San Jose supporter ran onto the field and punched Peter Withe in the head. With that unbelievable occurrence, the Timbers' substitutes joined the fracas on the pitch before assistant Leo Crowther managed to prevent them from engaging in additional fighting. Toplak was cautioned, but nothing was done about the pitch invasion.

Just two minutes from time, a strange combination of shots, rebounds and deflections found San Jose its match-winner. Art Welch blasted a shot that was saved by Timbers' keeper Graham Brown. But Brown could not hold on to the ball, giving substitute Roboostoff a chance of his own. Brown again blocked the shot, but the ball bounced over the sprawling keeper and toward the goal line. Ray Martin tried to clear, but he could not make solid contact as Mitić swept in to poke it into the net for an Earthquakes victory.

The Timbers were devastated to lose in such a way but found their exit from the stadium no easier than the overly physical match. More San Jose fans invaded the pitch, one of whom punched Mick Hoban as the Timbers tried to move through the crowd. The visitors had beer cans thrown at them both exiting the field and leaving the stadium for the bus. "This is bush league in San Jose. This is certainly an intolerable situation, and I will be talking to the league about it," ranted Don Paul in a phone interview with the *Oregonian* after the game. Crowe added afterward, "I'm ashamed to be associated with this type of atmosphere."

Ultimately, the Timbers' front office decided not to press for league action on the San Jose match, choosing to use their play going forward as an answer to the antics at Spartan Stadium. Measured as ever, Leo Crowther took over training for Crowe while the latter cooled off. Crowther gave the official reason for the Timbers' decision not to ask for league penalties against the Earthquakes, saying, "We cannot turn this into a grudge because that would harm our team play. I don't expect to see our return game there to be a revenge match."

More important than possible revenge against San Jose was the fact that the Timbers lost the game with a man advantage and lost Brian Godfrey and Tony Betts to injuries. Mick Hoban was forced back from a thigh injury to replace Godfrey when the latter left the game in the first half with a pulled hamstring. Hoban played well but got a yellow card of his own just after the hour mark. Betts was substituted in the second half due to a calf injury and was replaced by Donald Gardner, making his first appearance since the season's earliest games. With home matches four and seven days later against Dallas Tornado and San Antonio Thunder, respectively, the Timbers could not afford injuries to key players.

4

The Winning Streak

Luckily for Portland, its next opponent was Dallas Tornado, which suffered from severe injury woes in the early part of the season. The Timbers' front office could also count on high attendance, despite the recent loss to San Jose, due to the arrival of television star and famous American soccer player Kyle Rote Jr. The twenty-five-year-old forward, and son of the notable American football player of the same name, was a 1972 draft pick of Dallas Tornado. Dallas owner Lamar Hunt brought Rote Jr. into the NASL with the hopes of making him a household name across America. Rote Jr. led the league in scoring in 1973, winning Rookie of the Year and earning the moniker "Great American Hope." Rote Jr. even had a *Sports Illustrated* article devoted to him in August 1973 as Dallas reached the league final before losing to the Philadelphia Atoms. But the young player became nationally famous for an entirely different reason.

In 1973, ABC premiered a two-hour special called *Superstars*. The gist of the show was to have famous athletes from different sports compete against one another in various sports outside their own expertise. The show was such a success that the network brought it back in 1974 with new athletes. One of those involved was Kyle Rote Jr. The soccer star outlasted the likes of O.J. Simpson, Franco Harris, Pete Rose and John Havlicek to win the 1974 version of *Superstars*, instantly making his name and face recognizable across a much wider spectrum of American sports viewers.

Rote Jr. was again successful in the 1974 season for Dallas, leading the Tornado to the Central Division title for the second straight year. Rote Jr. had fewer goals and assists than in his sparkling 1973 season but had become the league's only box office attraction overnight. In February 1975, Rote Jr. took part in the *Superstars* show, this time falling short, finishing third. Prior to the signing of Pelé in June 1975, Rote Jr. was by far the most famous soccer player in the league and could single-handedly double or triple attendance at away games.

The Timbers were well aware of Rote Jr.'s popularity and played up his appearance in Portland by advertising a special promotion in the week leading up to his arrival. The *Oregon Journal* ran a short preview of the Dallas match with the information most important to Timbers supporters: "Dallas, which features Kyle Rote, Jr., will show in Portland against the Timbers next Wednesday, June 18. A $5,000 sports car will be presented to the winner of a special penalty-kick contest at halftime." By June 15, the *Oregonian* was running an ad with exclamations of "See Kyle Rote, Jr." and "You may win this Fiat X1/9." In fact, Rote Jr., despite being a visiting player, was to draw a ticket stub with the seat holder given a chance to take a penalty kick to win the car.

Ahead of the match, the Timbers expected skipper Brian Godfrey to miss the game with his pulled hamstring, while Dallas imported Peter Creamer, a young defender on loan from Middlesbrough, to shore up a defense that had been devastated with three players suffering broken bones. If Portland was to recover from the loss in San Jose, Dallas was the perfect opponent. Pelé had made his New York Cosmos debut in an exhibition against Dallas on June 15 in New York. Not only was the Tornado short on players due to injury, but it also had to fly across the country ahead of its clash with the Timbers in Portland.

The day before the Dallas game, the *Oregon Journal* ran a UPI wire report declaring European managers steadfast in their lack of concern over the Pelé and Eusébio[12] signings in the NASL. "The players who have signed are at the end of their careers. I cannot see many young players following suit at present. The money may be very good, but there is no substitute for playing in the best company, at the highest level," declared England manager Don Revie. Such strong comments were made more interesting by the fact that most of Portland's team were in fact young players from English clubs, more than a third of whom were playing for clubs in the First Division, certainly the "best company" noted by Revie.

The combination of success in its three previous home games and the appearance Kyle Rote Jr. brought a club record 14,688 fans into Civic Stadium to see the Timbers host Dallas on June 18. Nearing 15,000 in attendance was surely a dream come true for the Timbers' front office, easily eclipsing the standing record of 11,335, set just eleven days prior against Vancouver and nearly doubling the projected average of 8,000 the club had set out before the season started.

Considering the Tornado's travel schedule, its injury issues and the Timbers' desire to get back to winning after their San Jose debacle, the result of the first half hour could hardly have been surprising. Barry Powell and Tony Betts scored goals within two minutes of each other to give Portland an insurmountable lead. Powell's goal was unassisted as he blasted a thirty-five-yard screamer past helpless Dallas keeper Ken Cooper. Betts followed 119 seconds later when he rifled his own shot past Cooper for a 2–0 lead. Betts took advantage of the extra playing time with a stunning display, overhead kicking the ball neatly over the defender's head before slamming his shot directly at Cooper. The Dallas keeper slowed the ball, but not enough to prevent it from bouncing over the goal line and into the score sheet. The Timbers could not have asked more of their midfield, despite the loss of Godfrey to injury. Betts plugged into the left midfield and McLaren dropped deeper, giving Portland even more of an attacking threat. By half time, the game was all but won for the Timbers, just in time for the all-important raffle drawing by Rote Jr. and the potential giving away of a Fiat sports car.

The car itself was a bit of a joke within the Timbers' front office leading up to the Dallas game. "That started and ended with Don Paul," remembers Dennis O'Meara. "So we drew somebody's seat number to take a penalty, to get the car. We brought somebody down, and she shot four feet wide of the goal! It was an open net, and she missed the goal entirely," the Timbers PR man recalls.

After the failed attempt for the Fiat convertible, the club rolled the car back off the field and allowed the players to return for the second half. It turned out that the second half was nearly as memorable as the half-time fiasco. Two Dallas players were sent off with straight red cards. Defender Albert Jackson went off in the sixty-third minute for kneeing Withe in the groin, and longtime Tornado forward Mike Renshaw was ejected in the seventy-seventh minute for a flagrant trip on Graham Day. The Timbers took advantage of the two-man advantage, adding a third goal in the ninetieth minute when Jimmy Kelly chipped a shot from a Barry Lynch assist. Dallas manager Ron Newman had to be restrained after charging referee Bill Miller, demanding an explanation for the dual ejections. Yet the score stood at 3–0, with Graham Day mostly responsible for shutting down Rote Jr.

The victory was the sixth in nine games for Portland and its fifth consecutive at home. The win also took the Timbers from fifth place in the Western Division to third, skipping past both Los Angeles and San Jose. The NASL's practice of awarding six points for a victory and an additional point for every goal scored up to three meant that the Timbers cleared the full nine points from their Dallas win. Though Portland sat fifteen points short of Vancouver and twenty-two shy of Seattle, the Timbers had also played three fewer games than their Northwest rivals, leaving the potential for twenty-seven points to be gained over the course of the season.

Just three days later, Portland entertained fellow expansion side San Antonio Thunder for the only time in 1975. The Thunder had a disastrous run of form and injuries leading to the sacking of manager Alex Perolli after only nine games (and a 1-8 record). Don Batie took charge of San Antonio and led the team to victory in its first game under new management, but San Antonio was hardly a good side early in the season, and the Timbers expected another easy win in front of a big crowd.

A crowd of 14,080 filed into Civic Stadium on Saturday, June 21, but the result was certainly not the same as the Dallas game three days prior. In fact, ninety minutes passed without a goal from either side. The Thunder relied on its outstanding goalkeeper, Sergio Blanco, who registered thirteen saves on thirty-six Timbers' shots. Frustrated by their inability to break through the overtly defensive Thunder, Portland nearly resorted to penalties to settle the matter. But with just thirty seconds left in overtime, Barry Lynch lifted a forty-yard lob toward goal. Blanco came to claim the ball but inexplicably allowed the ball to bounce off his chest. Willie Anderson, charging to challenge the keeper, pounced on the mistake and poked the ball into the net for his second overtime match-winner. Afterward, Crowe was furious that his team was unable to break through until such a late stage. "They undoubtedly were the worst team we've played this year," Crowe roared to the newspapers. "If you don't score early on a team like this, you never will."

Regardless of the circumstances, Portland completed their two-game home stand by winning both games and recording two clean sheets. The two victories also brought Portland back from the terrible loss to San Jose just a week earlier. Back-to-back away games in California against Los Angeles and San Jose came next for Portland, with a chance to pick up important points in the Western Division.

On June 24, directly in the middle of the Timbers' five-day break between San Antonio at home and Los Angeles away, Peter Withe was sold in England. Wolverhampton Wanderers sold the striker to fellow First Division side and local rivals Birmingham City. The Blues signed Withe for £68,000, the equivalent of roughly $150,000. Though the sale meant nothing in regards to his status at the Timbers, Withe's sale to Birmingham was a clear indicator of the success the center forward was having at Portland. The move also made Withe a new teammate of Ray Martin and a new rival of Barry Powell and the rest of the Wolves contingent at Portland.

Meanwhile, the Timbers were struggling through their first wave of widespread injuries. Brian Godfrey and Mick Hoban had previously missed games due to injury, and Graham Day due to suspension, over the first half of the season. But with the mid-point nigh, Crowe needed to test the depth of his side for the first time. Withe, Betts, Powell, Hoban, Godfrey, McLaren, Day and Kelly were all officially listed as injured, though only Kelly was assured of missing action. The winger suffered from prostatitis and was understandably bedridden. Day was also to miss the Los Angeles match after his ejection in the club's last away game.

The rash of injuries and newfound caution among the coaching staff and trainer meant that several younger players were likely to earn minutes for the first time since the opening games of the season. Prior to Willie Anderson's arrival, Donald Gardner had played significant minutes across from Jimmy Kelly on the right wing. With Kelly out sick, Gardner would be inserted back into the lineup, shifting Anderson to the left. Godfrey moved back into defense in place of Day, pushing Hoban to central defense and leaving the captain at sweeper. Betts replaced Godfrey in the midfield, as had become the trend for the Timbers. Yet Crowe even admitted ahead of the trip that Chris Dangerfield and Roger Goldingay could find minutes if some of the injuries to regular starters proved worse than expected. "They haven't had the opportunity yet, and I'm not sure what they are capable of. They might go in and do one hell of a job. They've earned a chance to show what they can do," Crowe conceded. With Betts due to miss the San Jose match, the second of the California pair, due to his fourth yellow card of the season, Crowe would even have to consider starting one of his other reserve midfielders.

Two factors seemed to contribute the most to Portland's injury troubles by mid-season: the Tartan turf playing surface and the English players' general lack of stretching and preparation. With a surface as hard as concrete, the Timbers suffered from foot and knee ailments throughout the season. The turf also caused terrible rug burns after any slide tackle. Ray Martin was especially susceptible to the burns, as he refused to stop slide tackling. To combat the rug burns, trainer Ron Culp employed a spray can that still

Mick Hoban in the Timbers' stark locker room, the starting point for banter between teammates and trainer Ron Culp. *Courtesy of Mick Hoban, personal collection.*

scares those Timbers players. Helping to prevent infection, Culp's spray would reduce the players to tears before scabbing set in. Often, scabs would rip back off with the next tackle, bringing Culp back onto the field with his dreaded spray.

While Culp's spray cans have lived on in the memories of Timbers' players, it was his dedication to teaching the British imports the value of stretching and training methods and his ability to relate to the players that had the greatest impact in 1975. According to Mick Hoban, "At home in England you kicked off at 3:00 p.m. and went out at 2:55. You literally did all your warm-up inside, and it was far from conducive for getting blood circulation. When we first came to Portland, we never stretched. Ron Culp said he'd never seen professional athletes so inflexible. We'd never done stretching, so his whole regimen was completely new to us." Due to his concurrent work with Portland's professional basketball team, Culp knew how to interact with high-level athletes. Though he stressed workout techniques that were unfamiliar and was responsible for holding players out who were injured, Culp fit right in with the Timbers. Hoban says, "Ron Culp was a fantastic trainer. Our guys loved banter. Ron, because he had been with the Blazers, understood that, and immediately the players fell in love with him."

Despite Vic Crowe's extreme reluctance in playing American players, Roger Goldingay, Dave Landry and Nick Nicolas did have some advantages over their British teammates. Willie Anderson recalls the trio taking better care of their bodies, both on and off the field. "They looked after themselves better, they were usually fitter and they were better educated than we were in that way," Anderson says. That dedication to training did not level out in terms of playing time, particularly over the first half of the season, but it seemed that the American-style training would have a longer-term impact.

While Culp worked out the Timbers in the hopes of being fit for the California trip, Crowe sought ways to contain Los Angeles forward Uri Banhoffer. The Uruguayan striker led the Aztecs with eight goals and four assists over the first half of the season and was one of just several holdovers from LA's championship-winning side of 1974. The Aztecs were difficult to scout because their manager was twenty-five-year-old Terry Fisher. With a team almost completely changed over from 1974 and a young manager with no professional experience, Los Angeles was a mystery to those clubs facing it early in the season. Crowe also had to balance his energies over preparing for Los Angeles and for the San Jose match the following day. After the calamitous meeting earlier in the month, the Timbers' manager was worried about stadium security, retribution by his own players and actively trying to plan a way for his less-than-fit side to win the games.

UNLIKE PORTLAND, LOS ANGELES IN the mid-1970s was full of professional sports to vie for the attention of Southern California residents. Amid the Dodgers and Angels playing baseball, the NBA's Lakers, the NHL's Kings and the NFL's Rams, the introduction of the Aztecs in 1974 was unheralded. As a club with a large percentage of Hispanic players and a home base of East Los Angeles College Stadium, the NASL's first Southern California club drew an average of fewer than 5,100 to their games in 1974.

Despite winning the NASL championship against the Miami Toros in its first year, the club was sold and moved to Torrance on the campus of El Camino Junior College. The Aztecs dropped from a twenty-thousand capacity to just over twelve thousand in their new environs. Additionally, the club traded seven Hispanic players to expansion side San Antonio Thunder, completely overhauling the team, and hired Terry Fisher as manager. The '74 side had been led by player-coach Doug McMillan, the NASL's Rookie of the Year winner. McMillan was reduced to the role of player only when Fisher joined. By mid-1975, the Aztecs were not nearly as strong as the championship side of the previous year, but they were competitive and hardworking. While attendance was improving, up to over eight thousand per game at Murdock Stadium, the Aztecs lagged behind their Western Division opponents. "The fanatic crowd support in Vancouver, Seattle, Portland and San Jose always made us envious in LA," says Fisher.

On June 27, the Portland Timbers faced the LA Aztecs with a litany of injuries threatening the normal lineup. Yet the Timbers were able to field nine of their usual starting eleven. Jimmy Kelly did not make the trip south, so Don Gardner replaced the winger opposite Willie Anderson. Graham Day was absent due to suspension, reshuffling the central defense and midfield as Hoban switched into Day's spot, Godfrey dropped in as the free defender, Tommy McLaren dropped back as a holding midfielder and Betts came into the left midfield.

Los Angeles found the first goal; Alex Russell scored on the hour with assists registered by Uri Banhoffer and Juli Veee. Portland regrouped and equalized just six minutes later as Withe headed in from an Anderson free kick. The header caught a deflection to beat LA keeper John Taylor. The score held at 1–1 through ninety minutes, and the Western Division foes went to overtime to settle the tie.

At the conclusion of regular time, Crowe was forced to substitute Barry Powell due to a worsening ankle injury. With Powell out, Crowe inserted nineteen-year-old Chris Dangerfield alongside Tony Betts in the midfield. Dangerfield had briefly appeared twice earlier in the season, but his inclusion in an overtime match away to a division opponent was certainly the most important playing time earned to that point. Rather than showing the nerves expected of a teenager, Dangerfield exploded into Crowe's consciousness in the eleven minutes he played in Los Angeles. The young midfielder blasted a shot within five minutes of coming on and played a vital role in the game-winner for the Timbers.

Dangerfield dribbled directly into the eighteen-yard box toward LA's goal in the 102nd minute. As Taylor approached to challenge, the midfielder slipped the ball to Withe, who banged in the match-winner. The 2–1 final gave the Timbers their fourth overtime victory in as many tries and registered an important division win. Dangerfield's insertion helped change Portland's tempo after a difficult 90 minutes. "I don't know why, but we looked sluggish the whole game," Crowe wondered aloud afterward. "I was pleased with Chris. As I said before the game," added the relieved manager, "I wanted some of the other lads to get their chances now."

Lost in the accolades for Withe and Dangerfield was the stellar play of goalkeeper Graham Brown, who recorded twelve saves. Under a barrage of thirty-two shots, Brown allowed just the opener and kept the Timbers in the game.

With eight important points earned in Los Angeles, the Timbers turned north for a rematch with the San Jose Earthquakes the following night. Withe, despite scoring both goals, was doubtful for the next game, and Tony Betts was suspended due to yellow card accumulation. The Timbers could welcome back Graham Day, but Jimmy Kelly remained sick back in Portland. Brian Godfrey's thigh injury had gotten the better of him, forcing the captain to sit out, and Barry Powell's ankle remained a major question.

Perhaps of greater concern for the Timbers was the expected crowd control for their return to Spartan Stadium. The NASL created a new directive requiring the home club to supply two security guards for every thousand in attendance in response to San Jose's inability to prevent pitch invasions in its first hosting of Portland.

Impressed with Dangerfield's performance the previous night, Crowe turned to the nineteen-year-old for a starting role with Betts suspended. Having played just eleven minutes also helped Dangerfield, as most of the rest of the starters had played the full game the night before. Don Gardner started on the right wing, marking the first time Dangerfield and Gardner had started together since moving to Portland. "We were close; he was one of my best friends," explains Dangerfield.

Official travel itinerary given to the players by public relations officer Dennis O'Meara. The combined visits to Los Angeles and San Jose represented the fourth trip away for the Timbers in 1975. *Courtesy of Tony Betts.*

The familiarity of Wolves teammates Gardner, Dangerfield, Barry Powell and Peter Withe was very useful for the Timbers against San Jose once the match kicked off. But before the game started, another strange sight added to the growing lore around the San Jose–Portland rivalry. Having been directed by the NASL to provide additional security, the Earthquakes continued their practice of pushing the boundaries between sporting event and circus.

San Jose debuted newly signed Jinky Johnstone[13] in the newspapers ahead of the Timbers' return match, posing with defender Laurie Calloway and Bombay, a tiger on loan to the Earthquakes from Marine World–Africa, USA, a tourist attraction twenty-five miles away. Though Bombay looked harmless, seemingly cuddling a soccer ball in the press photos, the tiger's appearance in the stadium before the June 28 Earthquakes-Timbers match was anything but reassuring for the visitors.

Roaming the sidelines and prowling around the players, Bombay gave quite a welcome to Portland. Ultimately, though the tiger certainly provided a spectacle, it did little to intimidate the Timbers once they stepped on the field—and Bombay was removed.

At the quarter hour, Portland struck first as the new, young lineup manufactured a stunning opener. Withe took the ball on the right side, directing a centering pass to Gardner, who was drifting inward from the wing. Gardner flipped the ball to Dangerfield, who volleyed from twenty-five yards. The blistering shot flew past debutant keeper Gary St. Clair and gave the Timbers the early lead. The nineteen-year-old could claim a game-winning assist and a goal in just twenty-six minutes in the weekend road trip.

But the Timbers could not prevent San Jose from finding an equalizer just before the end of the first half. A nice buildup from Johnstone, Ilija Mitić and Paul Child led to a Terry Lees goal from inside the six-yard box and a 1–1 score at half time.

Crowe made a change at the half, removing Powell and inserting Roger Goldingay in the attacking midfield. Powell had been limping badly throughout the first half, and Crowe later admitted that he never should have been on the field. "I felt he had no chance of playing, but he talked about it all day," the manager ruefully explained. Goldingay took the starting midfielder's place and became the first American to appear in Timbers green and gold. Though he did not find a place on the score sheet, Goldingay did get a shot off in an exciting second half.

In the sixty-eighth minute, the Timbers earned a free kick just outside the box. Graham Day, up from his central defense position, took the kick and lobbed it perfectly to an onrushing Withe, who headed home for a 2–1 lead. The seventh goal of the season for Withe was by far the team high and gave him three goals in the two-game trip. The piecemeal Timbers managed to hold on over the final twenty minutes as Graham Brown made several saves to maintain the visitors' precarious advantage. With just seconds remaining, as they had done in the first half, the Earthquakes built an offensive surge and got off a quality shot, hoping to equalize. This time, Brown was up to the task, making a diving one-handed save to give Portland eight points and second place in the Western Division.

Unfortunately for Portland, the win was a pyrrhic victory, as Powell was lost to injury and Willie Anderson was given trouble over the final half hour due to a gash on his shin. The wound took twelve stitches to close after the game, but Anderson, aware of the frailties in the team, refused to be taken off. Brian Godfrey's continued absence due to a thigh injury left the Timbers very thin ahead of a crucial match-up with the Vancouver Whitecaps back at Civic Stadium just five days later. Crowe considered using Godfrey in the San Jose match to maintain a modicum of experience in the lineup but instead relied on Anderson for that role. "We didn't want to risk Brian again, because if I keep doing it, we won't have him at all," Crowe noted. Ultimately, Crowe's gamble on youth paid off, which he acknowledged after the game, saying, "They went in and did reasonably well. That's good for our game—and good for them. You have to be able to use all your players." Another performance from the youngsters would be necessary with several more experienced players missing training ahead of the upcoming Vancouver match. Said Crowe, "Vancouver is the best team we have played, and some of our lads will not even work out until Wednesday. It will be a stern test."

With a 9-3 record and two different four-game winning streaks to their credit, the Portland Timbers were quickly becoming one of the top teams in the NASL. Average attendance had climbed above ten thousand through the first seven home games, and the Timbers' players were becoming recognizable figures in Portland. The inauspicious start to the season did not exactly lend celebrity to the players, apart from Jimmy Kelly, but six consecutive home victories attracted more support and more interest in the players themselves.

Indeed, as spring shifted into summer and the Timbers climbed the table in the Western Division, attendance grew. More new fans were exposed to a sport they more than likely had never watched before, and importantly, fans returned game after game, learning the nuances of the sport and further appreciating the Timbers' style of play. Coupling the winning with cheap ticket prices and accessibility that made the players seem more like neighbors than intimidating athletes, the popularity of the team soared. An increasing familiarity with the players, in large part due to myriad public appearances throughout the year, promoted a sense of community among fans and players alike.

While the Timbers were appearing all across the city promoting the team and the sport, post-game parties hosted by the team were social events without rival. Though they were not the only club in the league to do so, the Timbers' parties brought players and fans together in ways that could not be achieved by simple appearances. The Benson Hotel was most frequently the host of the social gatherings that included Timbers' players, opposing players, city dignitaries, fans and anyone else who could cram into the small lobby. Later in the season, the team hosted parties at the downtown Hilton Hotel, as it provided more space. "You could tell the fans loved it because

In the hopes of attracting families to their games, the Timbers offered discounted prices for children. This pocket schedule was printed before the change in schedule due to the replacement of Civic Stadium's Tartan turf surface. *Courtesy of Eric Berg.*

they were all there. You could barely get past the first group of people. The players enjoyed the hell out of it," remembers Mick Hoban.

According to Stella Terry, an early Timbers' fan and founder of the Timbers Booster Club in 1976, the post-game parties were a stroke of genius. "They weren't wild, rowdy sessions, but the team would be introduced and people would get to see them. They'd have a chance to meet the players, and kids could get autographs. It was a friendly, open atmosphere that was a wonderful opportunity for people to meet their idols. The players had never really encountered anything like that in the UK."

For the single players, the newfound popularity was a means to have fun and meet girls. Chris Dangerfield and Donald Gardner were the youngest Timbers, each just nineteen years old.[14] Barry Powell and Jimmy Kelly had each turned twenty-one early in 1975. Without wives or children to think about, the youngsters made a habit of enjoying the celebrity their status as Timbers players afforded them. But in Oregon, the legal drinking age was twenty-one. That limitation, especially when compared to the relatively lax drinking laws in the United Kingdom, left young Dangerfield in a quandary. His problems were solved in a typically Portland way, through the do-it-yourself work of teammate Nick Nicolas. Nicolas explains, "The guys had driver's licenses that didn't have their age in it or their birthdate. So I took it, and on an electric typewriter, put in his birthdate so he was twenty-one."

While the self-corrected driver's license got Dangerfield in the door at bars and clubs across town, not all of the players' wishes were so easily granted. After several weeks of living in Portland, the four single players from

Left: Brian Godfrey with Timbers Booster Club founder Stella Terry. An ex-pat herself, Terry set the stage for the Booster Club's 1976 debut by purchasing tickets in bulk for fellow supporters and becoming personally acquainted with the players. *Courtesy of Stella Terry, personal collection.*

Below: Nick Nicolas in his apartment at the Tall Firs, proudly wearing his training shirt and displaying various Timbers memorabilia on the wall. *Courtesy Nick Nicolas, personal collection.*

Wolverhampton requested a change in their lodging. Instead of staying in separate two-bedroom units, Dangerfield, Gardner, Kelly and Powell asked to be moved into one apartment. Once the team started winning, however, the youngsters saw the benefits of individual bedrooms. When the request was put to Vic Crowe for a return to their original arrangements, the veteran of many professional soccer seasons knew exactly what was going on and refused to grant his youngsters their own rooms.

Clearly, the players were having fun as their summer in the United States reached its midway point. With May and June behind, only July and half of August loomed for Portland. With two games in five days against division opponents, Portland could take over first place in the Western Division in front of its increasingly devoted fans. With an injury list growing by the day and a nine-day, four-game road trip just a week away, Vic Crowe needed to get everything he could out of the Timbers' two home games in the first week of July. The Vancouver Whitecaps were the first foe, a side beaten

Barry Powell, Donald Gardner and Jimmy Kelly outside the Tall Firs apartment complex, preparing for a road trip. Along with Chris Dangerfield, the four youngsters lived together in one two-bedroom apartment. *Courtesy of Chris Dangerfield, personal collection.*

twice already by the Timbers, but by the narrowest of margins in their last meeting. For their part, the Whitecaps were on a three-game losing streak. Still, the match was of major significance both in the division standings and in proving that the Timbers could continue to win while using substitutes.

Wednesday's practice, the last ahead of Thursday's game against Vancouver, saw Peter Withe, Willie Anderson, Barry Powell, Brian Godfrey and Mick Hoban all wearing team-issued tracksuits and mending on the sidelines. The extreme shortage of players meant that the Timbers had to enlist Dennis O'Meara, *Oregonian* writer John Polis and, of course, Crowe and Leo Crowther just to have enough men on the field to make training scrimmages worthwhile. Powell was the worst off, sporting a walking-boot on his foot, and was unavailable for the Whitecaps match. The only promising news on the injury front was that Jimmy Kelly was fit after his bout with prostatitis.

Yet the Timbers entered the match as favorites against the slowly sinking Whitecaps. The edge for Portland was plainly explained by Crowe ahead of the game: "If we're organized in practices, in travel arrangements and in all areas, we are likely to be organized on the field. I feel there are teams we play that don't know accurately what it is they're trying to do. I have tried to give our men a definite plan and goal." The statement was less a dig at Vancouver than touting his club's ability to stay on task. As it turned out, Portland's players would need to rely on every bit of training and discipline to pull out a victory against the visiting Whitecaps.

A crowd of 18,278 packed into Civic Stadium, setting another club record and the league's sixth highest total to date, with hopes that their Timbers would win the game and score three goals. If those two conditions were met, the Timbers would garner nine points and tie idle Seattle for first place in the Western Division. Instead, the first major activity of the match came

Opposite, top: Chris Dangerfield dribbles up field against the Vancouver Whitecaps on July 3. Donald Gardner and the Timbers' bench can be seen in the background, as can the second base dirt. *Courtesy of Chris Dangerfield, personal collection.*

Opposite, middle: With the famous Jantzen girl as a backdrop, Chris Dangerfield takes a free kick in the first half of the Timbers' July 3 game against the Vancouver Whitecaps. A lone British flag denotes a small group of ex-pats who watched each game from the east side outfield wall. *Courtesy of Chris Dangerfield, personal collection.*

Opposite, bottom: Tony Betts and Chris Dangerfield (13) celebrate the latter's second half goal as Vancouver's Les Wilson (7) watches. Betts scored the Timbers' second goal in a 2–1 victory over the Whitecaps on July 3, with 18,278 fans in attendance. *Courtesy of Chris Dangerfield, personal collection.*

in the form of a sending off. Ray Martin, Portland's right back, was shown red after just twenty-one minutes for kicking an opponent. Afterward, the defender cited retaliation and showed off a deep gash in his shin.

So the Timbers were down to ten men with more than an hour to play without their top defender. Not only that, Portland was without Barry Powell, Willie Anderson and Mick Hoban, each of whom was too injured to feature against the Whitecaps. Crowe was using Dangerfield on the right wing, Betts in the left midfield, Gardner in the right midfield, McLaren lying deep and Godfrey at sweeper. With Martin off, Crowe actually shifted his formation, an extremely rare occurrence. In previous encounters, Crowe had simply left the formation alone, shifting players within the system to compensate for the loss at the given position. In this case, the Timbers' boss dropped Jimmy Kelly from his left wing position back to a spot on the left side of midfield. Withe and Dangerfield remained up top, but the Timbers shifted into a 3-4-2 with Lynch, Day and Godfrey across the back and, from left to right, Kelly, Betts, McLaren and Gardner in midfield.

Though it took nearly forty minutes, the Timbers finally figured out a way into the net while playing shorthanded. Gardner, pushing forward from his midfield role, headed a pass to Dangerfield, who blasted a shot on goal from twenty-five yards. Dangerfield's low, bouncing shot deflected off Vancouver defender Sam Lenarduzzi and past goalkeeper Peter Greco for the opener. Ten minutes later, Godfrey lifted a free kick from fifty-five yards toward the head of Day. The defender nodded down to an onrushing Betts, who cracked the match-winner past Greco. Despite chants of "We Want Three!" from the home support, the Timbers tried their best to protect their two-goal lead and keep Vancouver from notching goals of their own. That plan failed in the seventy-ninth minute as Bruce Twamley arched a free kick over a leaping Graham Brown and into the Portland goal, pulling one back for the visitors. But the Timbers were able to pull themselves together and hold off Vancouver's late efforts and were presented the Columbia Cup afterward.

Crowe beamed after the match, showering rare praise on his players: "An unbelievable win before a tremendous crowd. I couldn't have asked for any more from ten players, anywhere, in any sport." Whitecaps manager Jim Easton lamented from the short side of the score line, "At times we played like we had nine men instead of eleven. Portland deserved the win. They are a good, solid side." The fifth win in a row did not achieve the necessary nine points to tie Seattle, but it did provide eight. With Los Angeles coming to town five days later, the Timbers could claim even more points against

Chris Dangerfield, Barry Powell and Brian Godfrey drink from the Columbia Cup after their July 3 victory over Vancouver. The cup was awarded after Portland won all three games against the Whitecaps in 1975 and was the first-ever trophy earned by the Timbers. *Courtesy of Chris Dangerfield, personal collection.*

a division opponent and make another run at Seattle. Success was coming from every corner for Portland as the 18,278 fans marked the fifth time in eight games that the club-record attendance was increased. Only a point out of the division lead with a game in hand, the Timbers' record was only behind the Tampa Bay Rowdies for top in the league. The players were even saying the right things to the local media, with young Dangerfield telling the *Oregon Journal*, "Getting into first place would have been nice, but we're thinking more of the long haul. All that matters is that we stay in the thick of things right now and worry about first place in the last few games."

Still, injuries were a major issue at Portland, and the knowledge that Ray Martin would have to miss the club's next road game, away to Hartford, meant that more positional rotation would have to be employed. Powell's Achilles tendon was not healing as quickly as Crowe would have liked, and the leg injuries sustained by both Godfrey and Hoban meant that the Timbers' usual substitution patterns could be difficult to maintain amid a long road trip. Expecting a strenuous two weeks ahead, Crowe gave his players three days off to rest and prepare for the most taxing stretch of the season.

THE THREE DAYS OFF FROM July 4 to 6 gave Timbers players a chance to enjoy some of the nearby tourist attractions without having to worry about practice or a stern glare from Crowe. Several of the English players and their families took to the Oregon coast over the July 4 holiday, while others traveled east to Mount Hood. As for assistant coach Leo Crowther, he was treated to a rare visit from his wife and daughter who had not moved to Portland for the season. Crowther was able to show off the environs, taking his family to see the snow atop Mount Hood in the middle of summer, as well as admire the cascading water at Multnomah Falls. In his own words, "We enjoyed a wonderful evening barbecue and marshmallow roast on the banks of the Willamette River and sampled the delight of sailing in a catamaran on the river itself, all courtesy of friends we had made."

Mount Hood was of particular interest to the British contingent of the Timbers. Rather than risking injury skiing, the players would occasionally drive up to the Timberline Lodge just to enjoy the views. Nick Nicolas remembers their first visit to the mountain, wearing jeans and T-shirts because it was hot in the city. Despite his suggestion that they bring warmer clothing, the players who ascended the mountain were surprised to realize how cold it really was. Still, the changes in topography and elevation were new and appealing to the British lads.

For other players, the beach was the highlight of summer, with Portland's proximity being particularly useful. Says Willie Anderson, "It was just beautiful. In England, you'd go to the beaches, and there were a million people there. The beaches in Oregon blew me away; there was hardly anyone on them."

No matter how the players spent their short break, it seems Crowe's plans worked to perfection. Though not all the players were fully healed in time for Los Angeles's visit on July 8, the mental strain of playing six games in nineteen days had been lifted. A relaxing few days and a home match ahead of the longest road trip of the season was a perfect antidote.

Sure enough, the Timbers came out firing against the Aztecs in their Tuesday night game. By the end of the first half, Portland led 3–0 and ran the advantage to four goals before Los Angeles could pull one back. Tony Betts got the scoring started for the Timbers when he headed in a perfectly placed chip from Chis Dangerfield in the tenth minute. Midway through the half, goalkeeper Graham Brown recorded one of his finest saves of the season, a one-handed diving effort to prevent the always dangerous Uri Banhoffer from leveling terms. Crowe later called it a brilliant save, citing the importance of the stop in keeping the momentum in Portland's favor.

Shortly afterward, the Timbers were forced to use a substitute in the twenty-seventh minute, as Ray Martin was briefly knocked unconscious. According to Martin after the game, "I was on the ground, and I never knew what happened because I was out cold for a bit. I'm told I got a knee to the face." With his shirt covered in blood, Martin added, "Everything just went black on me out there. I think I loosened a couple of my teeth." Crowe had been reluctant to use Mick Hoban due to injury woes of his own, but the clear need for a replacement for the woozy Martin required the services of Hoban. With Martin due to miss the following game anyway because of his ejection in the Timbers' last game, the timing of the injury was actually as good as Portland could have hoped.

Willie Anderson, back in the lineup after missing time due to the gash in his shin suffered against San Jose in late June, got back on the score sheet by delivering a sublime corner kick. That lofted corner found the head of Peter Withe, who nodded the ball cleanly past Aztecs keeper John Taylor for a 2–0 lead in the thirty-seventh minute. Just five minutes later, Anderson assisted on another goal as he sent a low cross into the box, just grazing Withe and finding the feet of Jimmy Kelly, who was rifling in from the left wing. Kelly hammered the shot from close range past Taylor, who simply could not keep up with the speed of the Timbers.

The second half started with Portland again battering Taylor's goal. In the fifty-first minute, Dangerfield volleyed a deflection directly at Taylor from thirty-five yards. The immediacy of the shot stunned the goalkeeper, who got his hands on the ball but was unable to prevent it from rolling under him and into the net for a 4–0 Portland advantage.

LA's young coach, Terry Fisher, had already made one substitution at half time, and the 4–0 deficit led him to make two more over the course of the second half. The Aztecs were completely stunned by the Timbers' offensive outburst, particularly after having defeated the New York Cosmos 5–1 in their previous game behind a Banhoffer hat trick. The Uruguayan forward did finally do some damage in the seventy-first minute as his pass was volleyed in by Juli Veee for the Aztecs' only score.

Fisher's recollection of that game is not exactly one of fond memories: "Horrible, hard turf; cold, old locker room; crazy, supportive fans; and a highly energized team with hard defenders, speedy wingers and strong center forward." He would have been horrified to learn that the Timbers themselves thought it was their worst performance since their early season debacle away at Denver. Brian Godfrey, who nearly punched Banhoffer in the face early in the match, described the win in the terms usually reserved for a bad loss, saying, "We just didn't get together as a team. There were a few gaps back in the defense." Likewise, Crowe pointed to breakdowns and lapses.

Still, scoring four goals was a first for the Timbers, and the fact that four different players scored for Portland was a promising sign for a club growing reliant on Withe and Betts for goals. Picking up nine points from the game also moved Portland into a tie with Seattle for first place in the Western Division while still carrying a game in hand. The Timbers had won six straight games and ten of their last eleven ahead of their East Coast swing.

Four Games in Nine Days

Prior to flying east for their four-game road trip, Portland had not traveled farther than Denver. When the Timbers left for Connecticut to face the Hartford Bicentennials on July 11, they embarked on their first and only cross-country trip of the season. Due to scheduling to accommodate all twenty NASL teams while minimizing travel as much as possible, every club played each team in their own division three times and each team in two of the other three divisions once. The Western Division and Eastern Division were not scheduled to play in 1975, so Portland did not face the Tampa Bay Rowdies, Miami Toros, Washington Diplomats, Philadelphia Atoms or Baltimore Comets in the regular season. Having already faced the Rochester Lancers and Toronto Metros-Croatia at home, the East Coast visit would round out the Northern Division for the Timbers, as well as close the Central Division with the trip's final destination in St. Louis.

Ahead of Portland's departure, Seattle got a goal in a 2–1 loss to Vancouver that lifted it above the Timbers by a single point in the Western Division. Portland held two games in hand and was set to face Hartford, a team rooted to the bottom of the Northern Division. But before the Timbers could take on the Bicentennials at Dillon Stadium, the team had to make the cross-country flight.

For most players, flights of any duration were an enjoyable experience, or at least tolerable as a means to an end. But according to Nick Nicolas, there was one Timber in particular who did not look forward to flying: "In

England they didn't fly; they took trains and buses to the different parks, but we flew everywhere. Well, Barry Lynch hated to fly." Lynch's teammates teased him by offering preflight life insurance policies, though the defender's fears were exacerbated upon the team's arrival in Hartford. With a choppy landing in a rainstorm, Lynch was up and out of his seat as soon as was allowed, easily the first to deplane.

Road trips for the Timbers were a combination of Vic Crowe's iron fist and the experience of seeing new and occasionally exciting places. Mick Hoban explains how the direct-as-ever Crowe dealt with travel: "On road trips, his watch was the time. If he said the bus leaves at ten, he'd sit on the front seat, have his watch, and as it ticked to ten, he'd tell the driver to go. I remember Graham Day once being late and running after the bus and had to find his own way to the airport. But that was Vic. When he said ten o'clock, we'd leave at ten."

There was also a lighter side to traveling with the Timbers. "We were all given a Timbers team bag. When we got to airports, we'd place bets on whose bag would come off first," remembers Roger Goldingay. Nicolas explains who won this bet most often: "You had to bet, and somehow Brian Godfrey's bag always came out first."

Bets were not the only games played while the Timbers traveled. Nicolas had his jacket stolen by his teammates upon arrival in Hartford. Appearing without the jacket of his suit, Nicolas drew the ire of Vic Crowe, who expected his team to dress well when traveling.

Having worked in the NBA since 1970, the Timbers' trainer, Ron Culp, was accustomed to life on the road. A trainer in Cleveland and Portland before the Timbers' first season, Culp traveled all over the country and knew the best places to stay, the best places to eat and anything in between. "Ron did everything on the road. He was the traveling secretary as much as he was the trainer," says Dennis O'Meara. Leo Crowther gives Culp the highest praise, saying, "Our nomadic lifestyle on the road would have been much more fraught with difficulties had Ron not been an integral part of our team."

As was the case in earlier games against Chicago and San Antonio, Portland's game against the Hartford Bicentennials was a match-up of two expansion clubs. Hartford was struggling in its inaugural season with a 3-9 record under coach Manfred Schellscheidt, a thirty-five-year-old German who had brief but successful experience at various levels of American soccer. After winning the American Soccer League's Coach of the Year in 1974 with the Rhode Island Oceaneers, Schellscheidt moved to the Bicentennials.

12 - Willy Anderson   13 - Chris Dangerfield   14 - Tony Betts
Forward   Forward-midfielder   Forward

PORTLAND TIMBERS

16 - Roger Goldingay   18 - Nick Nicolas   22 - Dave Landry   Vic Crowe
Forward   Defender   Goalkeeper   Head Coach

Vic Crowe   Leo Crowther   Ron Culp   Don Paul, Sr.
Head Coach   Asst. Coach   Trainer   General Manager

From the official set of headshots, the Timbers' coaches, trainer and general manager for the inaugural 1975 season. *Courtesy of Chris Dangerfield personal collection.*

In moving to the NASL, Schellscheidt brought fourteen players up from the Oceaneers to form the basis of his Hartford roster.

Despite having three members of the national team in the Hartford side—brothers Charlie and Henry McCully[15] and Kevin Welsh—the Bicentennials could not find consistent form in the league. Charlie McCully was Hartford's leading scorer by mid-season and the only reasonable threat to the Timbers' six-game winning streak. Portland arrived in Connecticut and practiced ahead of the game to get used to the natural grass pitch at Dillon Stadium. Just 2,582 spectators showed up to see the Northern Division's worst team host the Western Division's best.

It turned out that the biggest foes for the Timbers were heat and humidity in Hartford. Portland rolled to a 3–0 lead before allowing a late goal to win 3–1 against the Bicentennials. The full nine points from the victory pushed Portland past the one-hundred-point barrier, becoming the first club to reach that total in 1975. Tony Betts got his seventh goal of the season in the eighteenth minute when he headed in a cross from Willie Anderson. Anderson's assist came from the right wing, a lifted ball into the box, allowing Betts to run onto it and nod home the opener. After Crowe substituted Betts in favor of Donald Gardner just before the hour, Portland struck again. Anderson was the catalyst, sending a low cross into the box toward Peter Withe. The Timbers' center forward dropped to his hands and knees to knock Anderson's cross into the goal with his head. Graham Day got Portland's third twelve minutes later when he, too, headed in a goal, this time receiving service from the left wing. Jimmy Kelly's corner kick was redirected into the goal on a snap-header from Day in the seventy-seventh minute. The three-goal deficit was too much for Harford, and Portland subbed in Roger Goldingay for Kelly in the eighty-sixth minute. The Bicentennials did avoid the clean sheet when Reggie Clemenica scored in the eighty-eighth minute on a volley from inside the box.

The decisive victory was not necessarily the best-played game by the Timbers, though, at least according to Vic Crowe, who said, "We didn't play as well as we're capable of playing, but then when you play teams like this, your standard drops a bit. We missed a lot of chances to score." With another game the very next night in Boston, Crowe was worried less about the quality of his team's performance than the effects of the heat, saying, "I won't know until tomorrow night if the heat took a lot out of our lads. My hope is that we'll become accustomed to it. The heat and humidity were quite bad." Still, Portland left Hartford with a 12-3 record, tops in the league, and on a seven-game winning streak. The Oakland Clippers held the NASL record with an eight-game winning streak in 1968. A win against the Minutemen could draw the Timbers level with that record and keep Portland as the top club in the league.

WHILE THE TIMBERS TRAVELED TO Boston, Portland's American football team was set to begin its exhibition season in Birmingham, Alabama. The story of the Timbers' 1975 season would be incomplete without mention of the Portland Thunder, co-inhabitants of Civic Stadium.

The Portland Storm debuted at Civic Stadium a full year before the Timbers were in existence, finishing its inaugural season with a 7-12-1 record, good for last place in the Western Division. Nearly every club was a disaster financially, leading to the folding of almost every team in the league, including Portland. After the IRS impounded the club, new investors created the Portland Thunder to replace the Storm in the ten-team WFL for the 1975 season.

Despite the unsuccessful season, the Storm was an important part of Portland's sporting landscape in 1974. Young running back Rufus Ferguson was a star in Portland, and quarterback Greg Barton was promoted from field to sideline, becoming the youngest professional football coach in America at age twenty-eight.

Through the late spring and early summer, the Timbers' only local competition at the professional level had been the Portland Mavericks, an independent minor-league baseball team that also played at Civic Stadium. Founded in 1973 when the Portland Beavers club moved to Spokane in the Pacific Coast League, the Mavericks were unaffiliated with a Major League Baseball club and were owned by actor Bing Russell. Using Russell's connections and money, the Mavericks brought in a litany of former stars, including Bing's son, actor Kurt Russell, in 1973 and former star pitcher and controversial author Jim Bouton in '75. With baseball in full-swing and American football returning, Vic Crowe knew his Timbers needed to keep winning in order to draw crowds at Civic Stadium for the remaining NASL matches.

As THE THUNDER KICKED OFF its exhibition season in Birmingham, the Timbers waded through pouring rain in Boston. The Timbers were set to face the Boston Minutemen at Nickerson Field on the campus of Boston University (BU) as the skies opened and rain nearly flooded the pitch. The field was reconfigured when Astroturf was installed in 1968, better accommodating soccer and American football. BU was the second college in the United States to install Astroturf, so the Portland players had the advantage over many other teams playing on a familiar surface. But the rain completely changed the normal playing conditions, making the pitch

75

slippery and ill-suited for professional soccer. Still, the game was played, despite fewer than one thousand fans in attendance.

Boston was Northern Division champion in its inaugural season of 1974, defeating the Baltimore Comets in the playoffs before losing to eventual league champions the LA Aztecs in the NASL's semifinals. The Minutemen averaged 9,648 fans in their eleven home games at Boston College's Alumni Stadium in '74, nearly double the league average and good for fifth in the league. Boston had famous players throughout its 1975 season with American goalkeeper Shep Messing, Portuguese stars António Simões and Eusébio, Nigerian striker Ade Coker of West Ham United and German striker Wolfgang Sühnholz, recently of Bayern Munich.

Neither side managed much of a chance on goal in a first half dominated by driving rain and deep puddles. Boston opened the second half with Geoff Davies scoring a lucky goal. Alan Wooler and Simões drew Graham Brown out of the Timbers' net with a one-two on the right side of the eighteen-yard box. A wayward pass deflected off Davies and into the left side of the net, leaving Brown stranded and giving the Minutemen an unwarranted and unexpected lead just before the hour. After the Boston goal, Donald Gardner was again brought on for Tony Betts, changing the pace of Portland's attack. For its part, Boston substituted starting keeper Shep Messing in favor of Jan Michniewski in the sixty-seventh minute. Five minutes later, Chris Dangerfield took advantage of the change of keepers with a stunning individual display to level terms. The nineteen-year-old took control of the ball, dribbled up field, avoided three defenders and chipped the goalkeeper from fifteen yards. The goal was sublime, especially given the conditions, and kept Portland's hopes for an eighth consecutive victory alive.

Portland charged right back for its second goal just one minute later. Withe dribbled to the end line on the right side of the Boston goal before sending a sharp pass to Gardner in front of the net. The young forward put the ball easily past Michniewski, but the referee whistled Withe for offside. Though the Timbers protested the call, Portland and Boston remained level, denying Gardner his first goal.

In the seventy-sixth minute, Willie Anderson was called for a foul, giving Boston a free kick. Simões lifted the kick into the throngs in front of Graham Brown's goal and found Ade Coker's head. The Nigerian nodded the ball cleanly past Brown to give the Minutemen the lead and the game. Tommy McLaren, injured in the previous night's game, returned as a substitute in place of Jimmy Kelly in the seventy-ninth minute, but the Timbers could not find a combination to find a second equalizer, and the second-longest winning streak in NASL history ended at seven games.

Unreported until after the Boston game was Vic Crowe's absence at Nickerson Field. Assistant Leo Crowther paced the touchline for the Timbers as Crowe left the same day for England. The *Oregonian* originally stated that Crowe was back in England "reporting to English soccer management on the status of Portland's British players." This was clarified on Monday by the *Oregon Journal* as a trip to "smooth things over with English soccer managers regarding their players who have been injured while playing for the Timbers."

Don Paul, who had been fairly quiet since his outburst after Portland's first game away at San Jose, detailed the reasons for Crowe's transatlantic excursion, explaining, "Several coaches are concerned with their players being injured. Barry Powell, Peter Withe, Ray Martin and Willie Anderson all have been injured. Their coaches, naturally, are concerned over their playing status for the upcoming English season. I thought it was necessary that we get over there and handle it right away. We aren't hiding anything." Bill McGarry at Wolves and Freddie Goodwin at Birmingham City were the two managers most interested in speaking personally with Crowe. Clearly, the problem was larger than Paul suggested given Crowe's departure amid a vital four-game road trip. Had the issue been easy to solve over the telephone, surely Crowe would not have left the country.

Meanwhile, the Timbers were still only halfway through their East Coast visit with the trip taking them to New York next for the third game in six days. Unlike the trips to Hartford and Boston, Portland had several days both to recover and prepare for its first-ever match against the Cosmos and Pelé. With defeat experienced for the first time since June, the Timbers were ready to begin a new winning streak and enjoy some of the sights of New York City while they were in town.

After the Boston game, despite the loss, the Portland players and staff visited with the Minutemen at a post-game reception. The center of attention was Eusébio, one of the great stars of world football during the 1960s and early '70s. Eusébio was second only to Pelé in worldwide notoriety as a goal scorer and legendary figure, even in 1975. Though Eusébio had not even played in the game against Portland at Nickerson Field, he was by far the most famous member of either club. According to Leo Crowther, Eusébio held court at the post-game party much in the same way Pelé did whenever the Cosmos played.

The following day, the team could relax before its Monday flight to New York. For the players, it was a rare day off and a chance to get out from under the watchful eyes of Vic Crowe, who was in England.

The Timbers usually traveled with only players, coaches and Ron Culp. But on this East Coast swing, the team brought a television crew along for the first time. Dick Carr was the sports anchor at KATU-2 in Portland and the public address announcer at the Timbers' home games at Civic Stadium. His station, the local ABC affiliate, had decided to air Portland's game with the New York Cosmos on July 16 from Randall's Island. Carr, whose real name is Vic Karsner, joined the club on the flight first to Hartford and then on to Boston. "The only reason I went with them at first was to get some idea of how we were going to do this broadcast and what was going to be expected of me," Carr remembers.

All of the British players and coaches had preconceptions about what New York would be like. After a short flight to LaGuardia Airport, the team arrived in a city vastly different from the stylized version portrayed in the movies. The club traveled immediately to its assigned hotel—a Holiday Inn on Lexington Avenue. The environs were not exactly what the visitors had in mind ahead of their supposedly glamorous tie with the great Pelé and his Cosmos. "We never unpacked our suitcases as, in this hotel, the rooms were damp and musty," Crowther says of the team's initial accommodations. The players, though not necessarily expecting palatial suites, were stunned at the poverty surrounding the hotel, particularly in the heat of the summer.

The Timbers did not last long on Lexington Avenue. Culp, a veteran of travel with the Trail Blazers, knew enough of the city to give Don Paul a call and request a change of venue. Several phone calls later, the team moved to the Sheraton on Seventh Avenue across from Carnegie Hall, just three blocks from Central Park. Even in a nicer part of downtown New York, the Timbers players and staff found themselves in strange situations. A man wielding a gun warned Culp out of a hallway while several players spent the evening mingling at the hotel bar with a supposed mafia figure named Rocky.

With the hotel shift behind them, the Timbers needed to train ahead of their Wednesday fixture with the Cosmos. Monday afternoon led Crowther to choose Central Park for training, as Downing Stadium was unusable due to heavy rains. The team assembled in the park and played seven-a-side games to refocus attention on the Cosmos and away from the details of travel. During one game, Peter Withe and Tony Betts collided mid-air while attempting to head the ball. Betts dropped to the ground,

Portland's practice in New York's Central Park. This photo was taken just minutes before Tony Betts was knocked unconscious by Peter Withe and required an overnight hospital stay. *Courtesy of Chris Dangerfield, personal collection.*

completely unconscious, only coming to after several minutes. The team finished practice as Ron Culp did preliminary tests on Betts. On Culp's recommendation, Betts was admitted to a hospital to undergo proper examinations. Crowther and Culp were advised to leave the young forward overnight for further evaluation and testing, to which the members of the Timbers staff assented.

By the next morning, Betts was ready for retrieval, so Culp and Crowther returned to the hospital to gather the injured player. Betts wandered out of his ward having received brain scans and an electrocardiogram during his stay. The Timbers' assistant and trainer moved quickly to leave but were confronted again at reception with payment demanded for services rendered; $650 was required, on the spot, in order for Betts to be released in the care of the Portland Timbers. Culp convinced the hospital that the bill could be sent directly to the club, as the patient in question was indeed a professional athlete and a member of an organization called the Portland Timbers. Betts was eventually cleared to leave, the club was billed and the three bewildered visitors returned to their hotel.

With Tony Betts retrieved from the hospital, Timbers players joined assistant coach Leo Crowther on a tour of New York City. Here several players pose in front of Madison Square Garden. *Top row*: Tommy McLaren, Betts, Peter Withe, Nick Nicolas and Graham Day. *Bottom row*: Donald Gardner, Willie Anderson, Jimmy Kelly, Crowther, Mick Hoban, Barry Lynch and Chris Dangerfield. *Courtesy of Leo Crowther, personal collection.*

Rather than risking further injuries, as Betts was now unfit to feature in Wednesday's game, Crowther called off training and opened up the rest of the day for sightseeing. Despite his injury, Betts joined his teammates as they visited the Empire State Building, Madison Square Garden and other famous spots across the city. Several players donned Timbers T-shirts as the group of mostly British youngsters moved en masse from one site to the next, gazing upward at the massive buildings and taking photographs.

Later in the day on Tuesday, Carr and Crowther traveled out to Randall's Island to visit Downing Stadium and determine the best location for the cameras in regard to the television broadcast. "When we got to Randall's Island, it looked like an old high school stadium with the press box on one side of the field and all of the stadium lights on the other side. Had we broadcasted from the press box, we would've been on the wrong side of the field, and the cameras would've been shooting into the lights. It was a very old, quaint stadium," recalls Carr. The two determined that a card table atop the concrete risers, opposite the press box, would be the best spot for calling the game, despite the RFK Bridge passing overhead.

By Wednesday, the team was anxious to play again and ready to avenge its loss in Boston. The Timbers boarded a bus and made the five-mile trek to Randall's Island for the game. Upon arrival, the Timbers players entered the stadium, changed and warmed up for their first televised appearance in green and gold.

BACK IN PORTLAND, FANS OF the Timbers were anticipating watching the team on television against the New York Cosmos. KATU advertised heavily in both the *Oregonian* and the *Oregon Journal* in the days leading up to the game, reminding fans in large, bold letters that they could watch "the Portland Timbers meet PELÉ and all the New York Cosmos on TV!" The game aired in Portland at 6:00 p.m. on July 16, on a ninety-minute tape delay. Dick Carr was to call play-by-play and Leo Crowther the color commentary. Producer Wayne Brown was touted as having played soccer in college, and therefore had enough of an understanding of the game to instruct the three cameramen. The KATU crew even had a slow-motion camera for the game.

As for the Cosmos, the club was at that time not nearly as famous, nor infamous, as it later became. Ahmet and Nesuhi Ertegün, founders and executives of Atlantic Records, and Steve Ross, president of Warner Communications, created the New York Cosmos in 1971. Jorge Siega, a Brazilian forward, was signed as the club's first ever player in March 1971, and Bermudan international forward Randy Horton was added later that spring. The latter won Rookie of the Year in the club's first season and led the Cosmos to the 1972 NASL title, winning league MVP after scoring twenty-two goals in just thirteen games. Ross had been courting Pelé since the team's founding, even designing the club's kits to resemble the green and yellow of Brazil. It took a $1.4 million per year contract to finally lure Pelé to New York. Having played previously at both Yankee Stadium and Hofstra Stadium, the Cosmos were entrenched at Downing Stadium when Pelé arrived in June 1975.

Despite playing in North America's biggest city, the Cosmos had never averaged more than 5,700 fans in their four previous seasons and brought in just over 3,500 per game in 1974. Yet Pelé's inclusion in the side led to sold-out grounds all over the country. The 22,500 seats at Downing Stadium were frequently filled for the games the great Brazilian played, despite the rapidly deteriorating conditions at the crumbling stadium. Downing Stadium was built in 1936 as part of the Works Progress Administration and was host to the 1936 U.S. Olympic trials, with Jesse Owens qualifying on the date of the stadium's grand opening. The lights were added from Ebbets Field when the famous home of baseball's Brooklyn Dodgers was demolished in 1960. By the summer of 1975, the stadium had been host to myriad events, but none as consistently popular as Cosmos games involving Pelé.[16]

When the Cosmos hosted the Timbers on July 16, New York was nine points behind Boston for first place in the Northern Division. Portland was tied with the Seattle Sounders for first place in the Western Division. Both sides needed a win in order to keep pace in their respective divisions. The Timbers were without Tony Betts due to his head-to-head collision with Peter Withe in Central Park, as well as Ray Martin, who had pulled a muscle in the Boston game. With the match set to begin at 7:30 p.m. in New York, Dick Carr and Leo Crowther sat at a card table atop the east stand, ready to share the experience of the Timbers' battle with the great Pelé.

On a hot, rainy night, just 13,421 came out to Downing Stadium for the game. The third Timbers game in six days, coupled with new injuries on top of existing ones, left Portland vulnerable. Yet often it is better to play again very quickly after a loss rather than take a break to consider what went wrong. With the first loss in seven games coming just four days earlier, Portland's players were eager to show that their quality was better than the result in Boston indicated. Portland also had manager Vic Crowe back from England not long before kickoff.

The match turned in Portland's favor just before the half hour when the Timbers opened scoring through Willie Anderson and Peter Withe. Anderson skipped around the corner of the Cosmos' defense on the right wing and fired a cross toward Withe. The Timbers' center forward chipped his shot behind Cosmos keeper Sam Nusum, to give Portland an early lead and Withe his tenth goal of the season.

Having controlled much of the first half, corralling Pelé through the man marking of midfielder Tommy McLaren, the Timbers used half time to rest their weary legs. Yet New York blasted out of the break with consistent pressure and two headers that nearly equalized for the home side. The latter of the headers came from Pelé and was only denied a place in the net by the intervention of the crossbar. Later, the great Brazilian rattled the crossbar with a free kick from thirty-five yards. Finally, on the hour, Luis de la Fuente fired a shot from outside the box directly at the Timbers' goalkeeper. Graham Brown parried the ball, but it deflected off the post and back into play in the goalmouth. Pelé dove past Brown to head the ball into the goal and level the score at 1–1.

Pelé's goal brought the crowd back into the game as fans in the ground, and even those leaning over the guardrail on the RFK Bridge, cheered on their Cosmos. Yet it was Timbers' captain Brian Godfrey who determined the final outcome on Randall's Island. Nine minutes after Pelé's equalizer, Godfrey lined up a free kick thirty yards from goal. While waiting for the referee to blow the whistle to restart play, Godfrey noticed an opening in the Cosmos' defense. "I was going to play it to the left," he recalls, "but I noticed there was some confusion around the goal, so I just shot over the wall of defenders." That lofted shot caught Nusum wrong-footed and passed easily into the goal for a 2–1 Timbers lead with just twenty minutes left to play. From there, Portland packed in its defense, cut out the passing lanes for Pelé and outlasted New York to win the game.

Pelé lamented afterward that it was his team's worst performance since his arrival a month earlier, yet his comments revealed more about Portland's team than the inability of his Cosmos to produce a result at home. "What happened tonight was that we played Portland's game instead of our own style. We didn't make the passing game but just kept kicking the ball downfield, and they would intercept," Pelé said through a translator. That the Timbers were able to control the flow of the match with their manager having just returned from England was a testament to just how composed and comfortable the Portland players had become. Godfrey organized what was a fine defensive performance from the back four and McLaren.

Afterward, Timbers players hurried to catch up with Pelé in order to have their picture taken with him. Crowe, Crowther, Hoban and Anderson had met Pelé previously when he visited England with Santos in 1972, playing at Aston Villa.[17] Yet it was McLaren who was the recipient of Pelé's shirt after the game. The Cosmos forward certainly made it clear to the press that he had not played well but attributed that lack of success

Having defeated the New York Cosmos, players rushed to have their photos taken with Pelé. Brian Godfrey (6), Graham Brown, Willie Anderson (12) and Donald Gardner (10) squeeze into this shot with the world's greatest player. *Courtesy of Nick Nicolas, personal collection.*

to the defending of McLaren in particular. The white Cosmos shirt with Pelé's name and famous number ten on the back was a prized possession of McLaren upon returning to Portland, according to Jim Rilatt, son of McLaren's local sponsor, Bernie Rilatt.

Six points from the victory and two more for the goals scored also lifted the Timbers into sole possession of first place in the Western Division, untangling a tie with the Seattle Sounders. Yet the victory was quickly overshadowed by a looming problem with loan agreements. Crowe's visit to England had been an attempt to quell increasingly annoyed English managers and work out agreements to allow the Timbers players to stay stateside even after the start of the English season. As Portland left New York for St. Louis, the final destination of its four-game road swing, the future of the club's roster was very much in doubt.

Don Paul flew to New York to meet with Crowe upon the manager's return from England. Having spoken with Bill McGarry at Wolves and Freddie Goodwin at Birmingham City, as well as other managers, Crowe reported back to the Timbers' general manager about the status of the loan agreements signed by Portland players. As expected, the West Midlands clubs wanted some of their players back prior to the end of their loan agreements in order to start play in the 1975–76 season. That season was set to begin on August 17, the same date as the NASL's semifinal round.

NASL commissioner Phil Woosnam met with Crowe and Paul in New York prior to the Timbers' departure for St. Louis in order to clarify the league's position on such matters. In 1974, the NASL had created a rule guaranteeing loan contracts of players from foreign teams for the length of their NASL club's season. The ruling was set up to ensure that players on loan could not be recalled by their parent clubs at inopportune times, namely during the playoffs or championship rounds, as had happened ahead of the 1973 final between Dallas Tornado and the Philadelphia Atoms. With five regular players missing between the two teams, the league was embarrassed and strengthened its position in relation to foreign clubs.

While the English clubs that loaned their players to the Timbers were certainly welcome to voice their complaints, as far as the league was concerned, Portland would be in violation of the NASL constitution if it allowed its players to return to England before the end of the Timbers' 1975 season. That situation left the Timbers in quite a bind. Keeping the on-loan players such as Peter Withe, Barry Powell and Willie Anderson greatly enhanced their chances of reaching and perhaps winning the league final. But keeping the players longer than the parent clubs wished could harm the relationship between clubs for future seasons and could jeopardize the opportunity to bring in key players during future summers. If they appeased the English clubs for future considerations, the Timbers would be in violation of the NASL's rules and could face a heavy fine.

As Portland flew to St. Louis to prepare for its matchup with the Central Division–leading Stars, the prospects of losing players to English clubs intensified. The morning of the game in St. Louis, the *Oregonian* ran a story announcing that two unidentified players were very likely to be lost for the playoffs, though the club refused to reveal their names. Speculation that Peter Withe was one of the players in question percolated through league and team sources, though the second player was more difficult to identify. Barry Powell was the likeliest candidate, though both the *Oregon Journal* and the *Oregonian* floated Willie Anderson's name as well.

John Gilbertson revealed that he expected the Timbers would almost certainly lose at least one player and emphasized the importance of keeping on good terms with parent clubs in England, saying, "I think we'll probably lose one—but we're not giving up on that one either. We have next year to think about. We must maintain our relationship with these individual clubs. If we fought, we would win the battle but lose the war."

Preparing to play their fourth game in nine days in a fourth different city, the Timbers arrived in St. Louis to play the Stars. Along with the Dallas Tornado, the St. Louis Stars were the oldest club in the NASL, founded in the National Professional Soccer League in 1967 by Bob Hermann, now the namesake of collegiate soccer's most prestigious award.[18] The club survived the NPSL merger with the United Soccer Association and was part of the original twelve-team NASL in 1968. Over the club's ten-year history in St. Louis, the team varied its home stadium between Busch Stadium and Francis Field, then a ten-thousand-seat stadium on the campus of Washington University. During the 1975 season, the Stars were at Francis Field, where they averaged just 6,071 fans per game. The stadium was built for the 1904 World's Fair and was used for the 1904 Olympics.

The Stars were a strong squad in 1975, the best team to ever play in St. Louis during their NASL era. At 11-7 and well clear of the second place Chicago Sting, St. Louis was likely to reach the playoffs behind the strength of its goalkeeper, Peter Bonetti. The Stars had won just four and lost fifteen in 1974, so the success in '75 was quite unexpected. John Sewell, a longtime defender at Charlton Athletic and Crystal Palace, was player-coach for the Stars. Sewell won the NASL's Coach of the Year award for his work in turning around the fortunes of one of 1974's worst teams.

Francis Field was eight miles west of downtown St. Louis so the Timbers, upon arrival from New York, stayed in the suburbs. Similar to the situation in New York, the Timbers were not given a field for practice, so the team found an open area at nearby Forest Park for training. Absent from practice were Tony Betts, who was still recovering from the concussion suffered in Central Park, and Ray Martin. In addition to the pulled muscle in his leg, Martin had been granted leave to return to Portland and care for his family. The Martins were visitors at Crater Lake National Park during a period earlier in July when raw sewage had contaminated drinking water, leaving guests and employees alike sick with dysentery and other ailments. Martin himself was sick and had flown back to Oregon from New York.

Torrential rain accompanied an explosive storm and turned the playing surface at Francis Field into more of a pond than a pitch as the wet weather continued into Saturday. The teams kicked off amid deep puddles and did their best to play professional soccer. The Timbers got the first goal of the game when Peter Withe scored in the twenty-first minute. The early goal was important for Portland as the rain intensified and the surface deteriorated throughout the match. The score remained 1–0 through half time and into the final twenty minutes of the match.

Portland's lineup was quite different from usual, with injuries moving players into unfamiliar positions. Martin's absence brought Brian Godfrey back into defense, which in turn saw Chris Dangerfield slot into the midfield and pushed Tommy McLaren back into the holding role. This triple switch had been performed several times during the season using either Dangerfield or Tony Betts. But an injury to Mick Hoban in Friday's training at Forest Park left Vic Crowe with a dilemma. His utter reluctance to use defender Nick Nicolas as a substitute forced Crowe to ask the concussed Betts to fill in at the back, a position where Betts had never before played. "I had a word with Tony before the game and asked him to play there. He told me he'd play anywhere," Crowe admitted after the game.

Withe's goal stood until the seventy-fifth minute, when the entire game turned upside down. Graham Day, in an effort to clear a shot from near the goal line, crashed backward into goalkeeper Graham Brown, knocking both to the ground and leaving the ball bouncing in the six-yard box. A header from St. Louis forward Mike Seerey rattled the crossbar, deflecting down to the right of the goal, where John Hawley easily poked the ball into the net to even the score.

Just three minutes later, the Timbers were again victim to the combination of the poor field conditions and their own clumsiness. While trying to take a goal kick, Brown was called for a handball when he roamed beyond the box, the lines of which were no longer visible on the destroyed turf. The infraction gave St. Louis a direct free kick at a distance of twenty yards. Defender John Carenza took the kick and lofted it over the Timbers' wall and into the top right corner of the net for a 2–1 lead for the home side in the seventy-eighth minute. With just twelve minutes left, the Timbers were in danger of dropping their second game in three.

Of all the players to save the Portland Timbers, it was Barry Lynch who proved the hero late in regular time. The quiet defender came forward from his position as left back and was the recipient of a perfect, short cross from Willie Anderson on the right wing. Two previous passes through the middle gave Anderson space to send that cross toward Lynch, who was waiting just in front of the goal. A quick nod sent the ball past Bonetti and drew Portland even at 2–2 in the eighty-seventh minute. Lynch was so excited about scoring that he declared that he was dedicating his first, and only, goal of the season to his son, Lee Michael. Even Crowe, the normally rigid manager, could laugh afterward, saying, "Barry's still talking, and I don't think he'll stop for about a week."

Still, with the score level at 2–2, the game needed overtime to produce a winner. The two teams played well into the overtime period before a goal finally prevented a penalty shootout. Already successful in its first four overtime encounters of the season, Portland found a goal from another unlikely source. Overtime was nearing its end when Jimmy Kelly took a corner kick in the 112th minute. That corner was blown dead though, as the referee was trying to allow second-year defender Bob Matteson into the game for the Stars. Matteson was brought in to replace John Pisani, presumably for the pending penalty shootout.

Rather than sending the retaken corner kick into the box as he had done on the first attempt, Kelly laid the ball off for defensive midfielder Tommy McLaren. In the 113th minute, McLaren took Kelly's short corner on the right side of goal and blasted a shot past Bonetti for a stunning 3–2 victory. The only goal of the season for the Scottish midfielder gave the Timbers the maximum nine points, a successful close to the difficult four-game trip and a triumph over the Central Division's top team. The victory also all but guaranteed that Portland would qualify for the playoffs, though its position in the final table and whether or not it would get to host a quarterfinal match were not yet clear.

Crowe was effusive in describing his team after the game, saying, "A goal down late in the game could have destroyed many teams, but once again we showed character. This was a long, hard road trip and to win three of four is tremendous. I'm just delighted with these players. I don't think I've worked with a finer group."

Having emerged with another close win, their fifth in overtime, and completed their longest road swing of the year, the Timbers celebrated in St. Louis and departed the following morning for Portland. As was the case when eleven of the fourteen British players arrived at the start of the season, the *Oregonian* printed the flight number and arrival time for the team's return to the Rose City.

Back in Portland, the Timbers players disembarked at PDX as one hundred fans cheered. Crowe, Withe and Barry Powell spoke with the media, while Chris Dangerfield gathered handfuls of roses from the crowd. Autographs were signed as the team basked in the attention given to professional soccer in Portland. With four games left in the regular season, the Timbers sat atop the NASL table with a 14-4 record and a league-best 119 points.

Top of the Table

The threat of losing two of the team's most important players loomed over the club ahead of its July 26 match with the Seattle Sounders. Goalkeeper Graham Brown's return to the Doncaster Rovers seemed imminent, and Birmingham City manager Freddie Goodwin hoped to bring in his new signing, Peter Withe, as soon as possible. With the match declared a sellout by the twenty-fourth, the Timbers were to play before their largest crowd of the season and one of the largest in the NASL to that point. Despite selling just over twenty-seven thousand tickets to the game, even more tickets were requested. A standing room–only section was considered on the east sideline but was eventually declared unsafe, as cigarettes were deemed impossible to control while spectators stood on the highly flammable artificial surface.

Fortunately for the Timbers, several defenders were able to return after the long road trip. Barry Lynch, Mick Hoban and Ray Martin were all cleared to play, leaving Portland at its healthiest at the most critical point of the season. Portland led Seattle in the West Division by eight points with just four games left for each side, meaning that the result of the match would be vital in determining which team finished atop the division. The day before the game, Timbers general manager Don Paul summed up his organization's thoughts, saying, "Tomorrow, we'll really be able to call Portland 'Soccer City, USA.'"

Yet the Timbers struggled to corral the intensity of the night and channel it into productive play against the Sounders. First, Willie Anderson was forced

Portland fans hang a banner declaring Tony Betts's supremacy to Seattle player-manager John Best during their July 26 meeting at Civic Stadium. One of the fans is even wearing a Chris Dangerfield T-shirt. *Courtesy of Tony Betts, personal collection.*

out of the game with a groin injury, altering Portland's dual-winged attack and requiring the substitution of Don Gardner. With that move, Jimmy Kelly switched from the right wing to the left. Gardner was on the right, providing the exact formation used in their season opener against Seattle.

Next, Portland allowed an easy goal from Seattle defender Dave Gillett. The Scottish defender slipped between Portland defenders on a Paul Crossley corner kick and headed the visitors into the lead in the thirty-second minute. With a restless crowd and an early deficit, the plan of all but wrapping up the West Division was unraveling. Fighting between Seattle midfielder Jimmy Gabriel and Brian Godfrey and Ray Martin nearly led to ejections even before Gillett scored. Kelly took more than a few minutes to adjust to playing back on the left, and Gardner, who had been used sparingly over the course of the season, needed time to work into the game.

The Timbers were saved by a tricky combination between Kelly and Withe, a play that leveled the score and changed the outcome of the game and season. Rather than trying to beat Seattle's outside backs to the corner flag, Kelly stopped short in the thirty-fifth minute, cut inside and flipped a quick cross toward the goalmouth. Withe battled Mike England for position and lifted his bearded head just clear of the Sounders' defender's, powering the ball past goalkeeper Barry Watling. That equalizer lifted the Timbers after a difficult half hour and set the stage for a dominant second half.

"We murdered them. That second half would have been good enough for Wembley tonight," declared Barry Powell in the locker room afterward. Kelly and Withe had more to say about the score, but the entire Timbers squad played exceptionally well in the second half. All five of Portland's Wolverhampton-based players were on the pitch together, and the passing combinations and shooting opportunities reflected that deep familiarity. Though the Timbers were well known as a crossing team, particularly from the wingers in to Withe, the personnel on the field gave Portland a slightly different attack. "We wound up playing the ball more from player to player instead of just in the air," Crowe explained.

Yet it was still a Jimmy Kelly cross that led to a Peter Withe goal that won the game for Portland. The Northern Irish winger got all the way to the corner and arced a ball high across the box. Withe and Gardner were matched up with England and Gillett to determine where and how the ball came down. It was Withe who first reached Kelly's cross, touching the ball down and then blasting a shot off the volley for a 2–1 lead in the fifty-eighth minute.

From there, the Timbers needed simply to hold their lead. Tommy McLaren was vitally important in that regard, stifling Gabriel in the center of the park to the point where Seattle manager John Best was forced to replace his exhausted midfielder. Meanwhile, Kelly repeatedly fired shots toward Watling and the Sounders' goal. Only inches separated Portland from adding to their slim but secure lead.

As the final whistle blew, the relieved crowed rejoiced. The Timbers players embraced before celebrating the important win with a victory lap. "It was a spontaneous thing," said Withe after the game. "The boys felt we owed the people something for the way they supported us. They made it feel like a championship game." Powell emphasized the Timbers' desire to win the game, saying, "We just had to win this one for the crowd. They really made the game." The official tally came to 27,310 fans at Civic Stadium, the largest-ever crowd in NASL history in a game that did not feature Pelé. The game was also the first sellout at Civic Stadium for any sporting event in ten years.

For perspective on just how important the Timbers had become in town, the World Football League's Portland Thunder played an exhibition game against the Philadelphia Bell the following day at Civic Stadium. With "Soccer City, USA" banners still hanging from the outfield walls, the Thunder played before 5,076 fans on a Sunday afternoon.

With just three games left in their inaugural season, the Portland Timbers were within two wins or two Seattle losses of securing the West Division and guaranteeing a top spot in the impending playoffs. Portland had also successfully convinced the NASL office to allow the Timbers' first playoff game to be at Civic Stadium, regardless of the team's final position. That decision seemed more than justified after the crowd of 27,310 on July 26.

Portland's final home game of the 1975 regular season came just three days after its victory over Seattle. The San Jose Earthquakes, the West Division's last place team by late July, came to play their only game in Portland. After two intense games in June, the Earthquakes' trip to Civic Stadium was a chance for the Timbers to win the season series and solidify their place among the NASL's elite teams.

Perhaps more important than the expected crowd of more than twenty thousand was the arrival of league commissioner Phil Woosnam in the Rose City. Several weeks of rumors, speculation and conversations across the country and the Atlantic still left fans, coaches and even players in the dark about the Timbers' loan agreements. Ahead of the San Jose rematch, Earthquakes defender Laurie Calloway spoke with the *Oregon Journal* about his experience on loan in 1974. Calloway was the first English player to sign a permanent contract with an NASL club when he returned to the Earthquakes for the 1975 season but had struggled to stay in San Jose for the entirety of his 1974 contract. Shewsbury Town wanted him back, but Calloway refused, citing his binding contract in the NASL. "I think it would be a good thing for the players, such as the guys in Portland, to make a stand now and insist on fulfilling their contracts here. I think that they could make it stand up," Calloway said.

Standing up for their contracts was exactly what the Timbers players wanted, though ultimately the decisions were out of their hands. By late July it was down to negotiations between Woosnam and officials from the

Football League in England. Having spoken with all parties, Woosnam came to Portland for the San Jose match in order to reveal to Vic Crowe, Don Paul and the Portland players the results of the negotiations.

Discussions in England and Wales[19] had moved beyond club-to-club negotiating and into the realm of each league defending its clubs and their stances. That did not keep individual club managers from expressing their frustration with the loan system in the NASL. "The NASL final is August 24, and it will be a few days after that before we see Willie Anderson. By then, we will have played four games. If that happens, I warn the Americans they'll be cutting their own throats. We will kill cooperation with their league stone dead," declared Cardiff City manager Jimmy Andrews.

Amid the accusatory remarks, the Timbers were still slated to face San Jose on July 29. Though the Earthquakes had been struggling in the weeks ahead of their final tie with Portland, San Jose had been a very problematic team for the Timbers in their first two meetings. Indeed, Boris Bandov set Portland into another situation of trailing early in an important game when his seventeenth-minute goal was fired in from thirty yards and deflected off the hip of defender Mick Hoban. The Earthquakes were unlucky not to double their advantage later in the half when Derek Craig rounded Brown and shot on what appeared to be an open goal. Only a last-second sliding deflection by Brian Godfrey kept the score at just 1–0 in favor of the visitors.

Due to injuries that kept Willie Anderson, Tommy McLaren and Tony Betts out of the starting lineup, Portland played with a starting back line of Barry Lynch, Graham Day, Hoban and Ray Martin. The midfield saw Brian Godfrey lying deep beneath Barry Powell and Chris Dangerfield. Don Gardner returned to the starting eleven as the right-sided forward, while Jimmy Kelly was on the left. Peter Withe was, of course, in the middle.

The lineup shuffle, particularly without Anderson and McLaren, kept the Timbers from mustering much by way of offense until the very end of the first half. In the forty-fifth minute, Kelly reached the corner and sent a short cross toward Lynch, who was streaking forward from his left back position. The fullback's shot was blocked, and the ball bounced fortuitously to Withe, standing directly in front of the goal. From there, Withe rifled a left-footed shot easily past Earthquakes' goalkeeper Mike Ivanow. That equalizer got the crowd of 23,005 back into the game and powered the Timbers into half time with renewed confidence.

Just six minutes into the second half, another Kelly cross found Withe in the box, where the Timbers' leading scorer was muscled down by Craig, resulting in a penalty for Portland. Powell stepped to the spot and blasted in

The Portland Timbers await the national anthem before their final regular season home game against the San Jose Earthquakes on July 29. Only Willie Anderson and Tommy McLaren, both of whom were injured and did not play, are missing. *Courtesy of Tony Betts, personal collection.*

the Timbers' second goal. "I figured he'd go right, so I pushed it the other way," said Powell afterward. Crowe was delighted to give Powell the chance to redeem himself on a penalty kick after his first attempt of the season was saved by Seattle's Barry Watling in Portland's opening game loss. "He's been waiting all year for that one. I wasn't worried," Crowe explained.

Despite the redemption of Powell's penalty, San Jose was not yet ready to capitulate. After each side made substitutions throughout the second half, it was the Earthquakes' Bandov who again found the back of the net, this time in the eighty-first minute. The twenty-one-year-old Bosnian had leveled the score and left the Timbers short of the points necessary to feel secure atop the West Division.

But the Timbers were not yet done either. Awarded a free kick less than a minute after Bandov's second, Godfrey lifted the ball toward goal with defender Graham Day as the target. Rather than heading on goal, Day flicked the ball back across the goalmouth directly to Withe. The star forward craftily knocked the ball between two San Jose defenders and past substitute goalkeeper Gary St. Clair for a 3–2 lead and another eruption of the large crowd.

From there, Portland was able to ward off the final San Jose advances and emerge with a hard-earned 3–2 victory and the maximum of nine points from the encounter. Both managers, though focusing on different aspects of the Timbers' season, agreed that Portland was in the midst of a special season. Said Earthquakes' boss Ivan Toplak, "Portland has the most experienced team in the league. Add good ball control and good running, and you've got a winner." Crowe meandered away from his usual analysis of individual player performances and instead spoke about the connection between the club and the community: "From the beginning, we built a relationship. We haven't been aloof; we've gotten to know the community. Some professional athletes act like they're gods. Not us."

Regardless of the inspiration, the Timbers were four points away from securing the top position in the West with two games to play. The final two home games of the season were the first consecutive games in NASL history to draw more than twenty thousand fans each, and the Timbers moved into third place in average attendance. With postseason play confirmed, only a short trip to Seattle and a flight down to Los Angeles were left in the Timbers' stunningly successful first season.

On the verge of a division title in their first year and among the league leaders in attendance, the best news of the season for the Portland Timbers came on August 1. According to a press release issued by the club, "The Portland Timbers will be able to retain all of the players on loan from Great Britain throughout the NASL playoff series. NASL commissioner Phil Woosnam said the players' overseas clubs have withdrawn their requests to have them return in time for the August 16 opening of the English soccer season."

With the services of six starting players guaranteed, including Peter Withe, Willie Anderson, Graham Day, Tommy McLaren, Brian Godfrey and Graham Brown, the Timbers were emerging as favorites for the 1975 NASL crown. In the longer term, the decision between the Football League and the NASL would be a disaster for the Timbers, but in their first season, all of the key components of the team were set to compete for the newly renamed Soccer Bowl '75.

In previous seasons, the final round of the playoffs was simply known as the NASL Championship. But with the growing success of the NFL's Super Bowl, then entering its tenth year, the NASL decided to give its title-deciding game a new moniker. Soccer Bowl '75 was the first of nine Soccer Bowls.

Before the Timbers could even think about playing in the Soccer Bowl, two away games remained on the docket. First, a trip to Seattle, Portland's first of the season, to determine the season series winner against the Sounders. The Timbers had lost their season opener to the Sounders 1–0 at Civic Stadium but had won 2–1 in overtime just a week earlier. The Sounders needed points badly in order to catch up to the Timbers in the West Division, though their inclusion in the playoffs was also assured. Portland entered the match having won four straight games since the Boston Minutemen broke its seven-game winning streak on July 12. Seattle, despite its recent loss to the Timbers, held the league's third-highest point total.

Such was the import of the final regular season meeting between Portland and Seattle that *Sports Illustrated* dispatched Pat Putnam to cover the game at Seattle's Memorial Stadium. Putnam was a famous boxing writer, having broken the story of Muhammad Ali's name change back in 1964. That this was the writer *Sports Illustrated* sent to Seattle spoke highly of the value of professional soccer in its pages. *Sports Illustrated* was not new to covering soccer, even placing Philadelphia Atoms goalkeeper Bob Rigby on the cover in September 1973. But specific attention to a single, regular season game was novel.

Putnam's record of the events of August 2 shows clearly the intensity and development of the emerging rivalry. The senior writer quoted Seattle manager John Best as saying, "Seattle playing Portland has become as heated as any neighborhood rivalry in England. It's Liverpool playing Everton. After they beat us, Portland celebrated all night. It was a victory for the whole town. And in Seattle, everyone has been saying how they'd show Portland who had the best team next time. It's what real soccer should be."

RIVAL SUPPORTERS STARTED THE DAY'S festivities by stealing one another's banners, fighting and chanting. The sold-out crowd of 17,925 set the stage for a dramatic and confrontational battle at the top of the division.

Jimmy Kelly got the scoring started in the twenty-first minute when he faked inside, cut outside and sent a cross toward a familiar target, Peter Withe. Kelly's pass was deflected by Mike England and floated toward the right side of the goal. From there, Withe ran onto it and volleyed in for a surprising Timbers lead. Having given up early goals in each of its past two games, Portland's early jump on the game changed the dynamic and forced the Sounders to fight back.

Seattle seemed to take the aggressive mentality a bit too far as fights nearly broke out first between Tommy McLaren and Tommy Baldwin, then between McLaren and John Rowlands and finally between Jimmy Gabriel and Brian Godfrey. Before thirty-four minutes had passed at Memorial Stadium, five yellow cards had been issued. But before Adrian Webster picked up the fifth caution of the match, Baldwin equalized for

Seattle. Hank Liotart[20] heaved a long throw-in toward Baldwin, but Mick Hoban was there to defend. Hoban was only able to get a piece of the ball, though, and Baldwin headed in to tie the game in the thirty-third minute.

Unfazed, the Timbers continued to bring pressure and in the fortieth minute appeared to earn a penalty. Rowlands grabbed Portland defender Graham Day by the neck and pulled him down in the box, yet amazingly the referee did not point to the spot or even blow his whistle. The failure to at least try a spot kick affected the Timbers as the brutal first half came to a close. When the second half started, Seattle dominated the midfield, a facet of its game unseen in each of the two previous matches. As if to punctuate the change in momentum, England fired a shot past Graham Brown in the fifty-seventh minute to send Seattle ahead, 2–1. From there, the game got away from the Timbers. The Sounders repeatedly battered Portland's defensive midfield and fired at will on Brown. Only diving saves from the Timbers' goalkeeper kept the score at a one-goal deficit for the visitors.

With Portland seemingly out of the game, Seattle was content to run out the match and keep alive its faint hopes of claiming the West Division crown. In the ninetieth minute, Barry Powell fired one last, hopeful shot at goal. That shot somehow managed to redirect off the back of Baldwin and carom directly into the net with just thirty-five seconds to play. Suddenly even at 2–2 and with the Sounders coasting, Portland had a realistic chance at stealing a win and securing the division title.

Into overtime the game went without much of an indication of who might emerge at the end. Portland was reenergized after a very difficult second half and immediately set to pushing forward for the match-winner. Yet it was Seattle that benefitted from another throw-in, this time with a graver impact on the Timbers. Paul Crossley lobbed a throw into the box, a ball that was allowed to fall between two Portland defenders and bounce directly to Rowlands, who slammed the ball into the net with his head. Seattle rejoiced, Portland sulked dejectedly away and the West Division remained up for grabs with just one week left in the 1975 season. The loss was the first in overtime all season for Portland following five successful encounters with the extra periods.

The Timbers hurried out of the locker room, barely speaking to reporters, before boarding their 11:15 p.m. flight back to Portland. A week to regroup was ahead of Vic Crowe and his Timbers, with one last regular season game to play down in Los Angeles.

As the Aztecs loomed in the final weekend of the Timbers' first NASL season, injuries—a problem that had seemed behind Portland just two weeks earlier—were back in a bad way. Five players were on the pitch with serious injuries, as neither side had made a single substitution in Seattle. Tommy McLaren required a cast upon leaving the Emerald City to help stabilize his injured foot. Willie Anderson was featured on the right wing despite his groin injury, while defenders Mick Hoban, Graham Day and Brian Godfrey all slogged through the rubber match with ailments that would have kept them out of a lesser game. Neither Ray Martin nor Tony Betts even suited up against the Sounders. Vic Crowe gave his team a rare day off in the hopes that it might expedite the healing process that would be necessary ahead of a tough tie in Los Angeles and the looming playoffs.

Despite all the injury woes, Portland could still wrap up the West Division if Seattle failed to score more than a single goal in their away game against the San Antonio Thunder in the middle of the week. Meanwhile, Crowe finished third in NASL Coach of the Year voting, with St. Louis Stars coach John Sewell taking the award.

The Timbers finally got good news on the night of Wednesday, August 6. A final score of Seattle, 1–San Antonio, 0 provided Portland the margin necessary to claim the division title. Though the accomplishment did not coincide with a victory on the pitch, the Timbers celebrated nonetheless. A party was thrown at the house of principal owner John Gilbertson; champagne flowed, and the players dove in and out of the Gilbertsons' backyard pool. The *Oregon Journal* ran a photo of Peter Withe head-butting Graham Day off the diving board and into the pool as the weight of the Seattle loss was lifted.

Seattle's one-goal victory in San Antonio also guaranteed that regardless of the results of the final match of the season, Portland would host the Sounders in the NASL quarterfinal round at Civic Stadium on August 12. In preparation for that game, Crowe announced that he would be resting as many starters as possible and said, "We'll play Dave Landry, Roger Goldingay and Nick Nicolas against Los Angeles. Even in this cruel, ruthless game which is professional soccer, winning isn't everything. Developing our players is important as well."

The news of a spot on the pitch was a first for both Landry and Nicolas, while Goldingay had managed an hour's worth of time over the course of the season. Crowe had never intended to use his required North Americans, but with the division title secure and a bevy of injuries, it was surely time to insert the three players who had survived his April tryout. Goldingay best expressed the sentiments of the trio of North Americans ahead of the match in Los Angeles, saying, "I've never had experience on the bench before, it's not easy. But our regulars are tremendous, and I have improved a great deal just being on the club."

Meanwhile, tickets to the Timbers-Sounders rematch at Civic Stadium in the quarterfinal round of the playoffs went on sale August 8 at 9:00 a.m. at eight locations around the Portland area. By noon, all eight outlets were sold out. Even with an additional 2,300 seats added with temporary bleachers, roughly 27,000 tickets had been purchased by the clamoring Portland public. That same day, the Timbers flew to Los Angeles to face the Aztecs in the 1975 regular season finale.

While Portland had already qualified for the playoffs, the Aztecs still had a reason to play their regulars in the last game of the season. The Vancouver Whitecaps and the Chicago Sting both stood to challenge the Aztecs for the final playoff position, with the triumphant side of those three facing Central Division champions the St. Louis Stars in the quarterfinals. With that in mind, the Aztecs struck first with a goal in the twenty-first minute, compliments of defender Bobby Sibbald. The score came from a rebounded free kick and gave Los Angeles a 1–0 lead at Murdock Stadium.

Crowe fielded a team featuring five substitutes, including both Roger Goldingay and Dave Landry. But a last-minute switch left defender Nick Nicolas out of the lineup in his only opportunity to play. With Brian Godfrey arriving hung over on the day of the game, Crowe was furious, and rather than allowing Nicolas to start in defense, the Timbers' manager forced Godfrey to play. While Nicolas sat, yet again, Godfrey managed three shots but had very little impact on what was a meaningless match for Portland.

After struggling through the first half, the Timbers finally found their footing in an exciting second half. Chris Dangerfield took control of the Portland attack, firing repeatedly on John Taylor's goal. Early in the second half, Dangerfield rattled the crossbar while Taylor managed a scrambling save in the game's dying moments to deny the Timbers' teenager an equalizer. All told, the Aztecs' goalkeeper recorded a dozen saves, eight of them in the second half. The 1–0 loss for the Timbers was their second straight and only the second time an opponent held them scoreless. The victory for Los Angeles earned the fourth and final playoff position, leaving Vancouver and Chicago out of luck.

Still, the Timbers were headed to the playoffs in their first year. With the Philadelphia Atoms in 1973 and the Los Angeles Aztecs in 1974 as examples, Portland hoped to be the third consecutive expansion side to win the NASL title. Crowe expected nearly all of his usual starters to return for the fourth game of the season against the Seattle Sounders.

Do You Know the Way to San Jose?

On August 12, 1975, the Portland Timbers played their first playoff game. It was their fourth game of the season against local rivals the Seattle Sounders and their third meeting in sixteen days. Though it was the quarterfinal round, the match loomed as the biggest of the season for the Timbers. "This has more significance for me than any game I've ever played in. Playing and winning Tuesday night would give me the biggest thrill I've ever had in soccer," said Ray Martin the day before the crucial derby.

When the day arrived for the Timbers-Sounders rematch, three thousand bleacher seats were made available at the stadium. Those tickets came in addition to the twenty-seven thousand already sold the week before. The game was televised on KATU, and the gates opened at 5:30 p.m., two hours before kickoff.

By the time the game started, an NASL playoff record crowd of 31,523 was standing in Civic Stadium. Nearly 2,000 of those in attendance were traveling Seattle supporters, while the rest of the overflow audience waved banners proclaiming, "Jimmy Kelly for Mayor!" and chanted "We're number one!" The previous NASL record for a playoff encounter had been the 18,824 at Texas Stadium for the 1973 NASL championship. Even other sports in Portland had not topped 30,000 since the 1965 Oregon-Washington football game, the last played at Civic Stadium. Regardless of the result of the game, Portland was host to the biggest and loudest game in league history.

Do You Know the Way to San Jose?

The first half between the Northwest rivals was similar to the first two encounters, with a thorough domination in the midfield by the Timbers. Barry Powell had perhaps the best chance with a rip of a shot from outside the box, but the ball narrowly missed, wide right, and the score remained 0–0 into the half-time break.

Portland was certainly the beneficiary of the meaningless final regular season game against Los Angeles because nearly every regular starter was back in the eleven against the Sounders. Only Mick Hoban was forced to sit due to injury, with Brian Godfrey filling in as a central defender. Tommy McLaren was able to return to the holding midfield role where he so consistently performed, while Powell and Chris Dangerfield were the explosive, forward-thinking midfielders below the usual top three.

After a comprehensive first half effort, the Timbers were stunned just four minutes into the second half when John Rowlands, the same player who had defeated Portland just ten days earlier in Seattle, shot past Graham Brown after a nice feed from Paul Crossley. That Sounders goal in the forty-ninth minute meant the Timbers would have to chase a goal simply to force overtime, let alone win the game in regulation.

Down a goal on its home field in a knockout game, Portland started to shoot. Though the trend started in the first half, the Timbers exploded offensively in the Seattle end of the field. Thirty-eight shots were fired, forcing a dozen saves and keeping the Sounders pinned into their own half. Peter Withe led the Timbers with eight shots, and though none ultimately found its way into the net, his presence looming in front of goal certainly distracted the Seattle defenders. Mike England was again called into service to mark the Timbers' leading scorer, but double and triple coverage on Withe allowed openings for others.

Finally, in the seventy-first minute, a Timbers' shot found its way past Watling. Withe took the ball by himself, a less common occurrence than his usual role in the box, and dribbled to the byline. From there, he sent a short cross back into the box with an onrushing Powell as his target. Without a chance to play the ball down to his powerful feet, Powell channeled his best Withe impersonation and knocked the ball on with his head. Watling dove to his left, barely tipping the ball on his way to ground. Before he landed, though, Watling's trailing arm nudged the ball backward into the net. Civic Stadium erupted as Powell and Withe celebrated together, and the game drew level at 1–1.

Nineteen furious minutes passed without either side able to find a way past the NASL's top two goalkeepers, and overtime was required, yet again.

Unlike the previous encounter at Memorial Stadium, the quarterfinal match was a clean affair. Only a yellow card for Arfon Griffiths in the first half left a blemish on the score sheet. The game had lived up to the hype, and the additional sudden death period had not yet begun.

The only substitution of the game for Portland came when Vic Crowe removed Dangerfield from the midfield and replaced him with Tony Betts. Betts was set to come on near the seventieth minute as an offensive catalyst, but Powell's goal kept the substitution from being made at that time. Though Dangerfield was frustrated, Crowe had his reasons for the move. "It had nothing to do with Chris's play. He was simply tired. I put in Tony because he liked to go farther downfield, and that makes him more of a scoring threat," the Timbers' manager explained after the game.

With overtime ahead, both teams went to their respective benches to rest. Several Timbers, including Brian Godfrey and Barry Lynch, sat on the pitch as Crowe moved among them, giving words of encouragement. Bench players like Nick Nicolas and Roger Goldingay patted their teammates on the shoulders as the Timbers' side of the field exuded confidence.

For a large portion of the overtime period, Portland controlled possession deep in the Sounders' end of the field yet could not achieve more than a handful of shots. Finally, the Timbers won a corner kick on the left side of the field. Willie Anderson took the kick, a ball aimed for Withe and Betts but deflected out by the Sounders. A poor clearance and the Timbers' pressure saw the ball passed between Tommy McLaren, Betts and Anderson and finally settled by Jimmy Kelly.

The diminutive winger looked up, just outside the dirt patch representing first base, and could see Withe completely open, jumping up and down, calling for the ball. Yet Kelly was patient and sent a through ball back down the line for Anderson, deep into the left corner. Anderson ran on to the pass as three Seattle defenders rushed to defend Withe directly in front of the goal. But Anderson had not crossed to Withe. He had, in fact, lobbed the ball back about five yards to Betts, who had reentered the fray after helping corral the loose ball just seconds before. Anderson's cross came directly to Betts, who ran on to the pass and headed the ball perfectly, straight ahead, just above the reach of Watling and just beneath the crossbar.

The string of set pieces, passes and goal took exceptional skill and a great familiarity to produce. Perhaps that is why, afterward, the Sounders players and coaches were not distraught. They realized they had been beaten on an exchange of pure class.

Tony Betts, donning the Timbers' V-neck Adidas home uniform. In its first season, Portland also featured a green crew-neck shirt and a white mesh crew-neck jersey, both made by Jelenk. *Courtesy of Tony Betts, personal collection.*

The crowd of 31,523 was not so shy about expressing their admiration for the match-winner from Betts. Fans poured onto the field, carrying decades' worth of Portland sports frustration with them over the walls. Thousands descended to the pitch and surrounded the Timbers, lifting Betts onto their shoulders and carrying him away with glee. Armed with "Soccer City, USA" banners and more write-in suggestions for Kelly as a mayoral candidate, the Timbers' fans celebrated.

In the locker room, Crowe beamed, having overcome the odds to reach the NASL semifinal round. "These are great lads. It seems like we've been together for years, and it's only been a couple of months," he said, sharing a sentiment widely held among the players. Ray Martin added a further explanation for the Timbers' resiliency, saying, "Talent wise, we're both very even sides. But Vic has drilled us and drilled us. We're organized, we know what to do."

Indeed, the Timbers thought that the Seattle Sounders were their toughest obstacle in their aim to bring the Soccer Bowl trophy to Portland. Yet there was another game left to play before the Timbers could reach the championship round. The St. Louis Stars, which Portland had defeated 3–2 in overtime in July, beat the Los Angeles Aztecs with penalties in their quarterfinal tie, leaving the West and Central Division champions to vie for a place in Soccer Bowl '75.

Three o'clock in the afternoon on Sunday, August 17, was the date set for the NASL semifinal between the Portland Timbers and the St. Louis Stars. Season ticket holders were able to purchase tickets ahead of the public offering, which began at 9:00 a.m. on Friday, August 15. All eight ticket booths were open and were prepared for an onslaught of Timbers fans wishing to see the final home game of the 1975 season.

The first Timbers fan to arrive to wait in line to purchase his tickets was Joe Dixon, who showed up at 12:10 p.m. on Thursday. Dixon rode into town on the bus from Redland. As the hours passed on the afternoon of the fourteenth, hundreds more arrived, many under the age of thirty and many from towns outside Portland. They came with lawn chairs, blankets, picnics and beer and created a carnival atmosphere outside the stadium. Meanwhile, workers hurriedly replanked a section on condemned, wooden bleachers in centerfield in preparation for a crowd of at least thirty-three thousand.

As she had done prior to the quarterfinal round, city councilwoman Mildred Schwab helped round up extra sets of freestanding bleachers and had them temporarily installed behind the south goal and along the east sideline, below the outfield wall. The two thousand extra seats came from parks throughout the city, at the expense of the city, to accommodate the record crowd. For those unable to squeeze into Civic Stadium on game day, KATU broadcasted the match live on television, while KOIN aired the game live on radio.

While fans waited in line to purchase their tickets, the Timbers practiced inside Civic Stadium on Friday. With training nearly over, Vic Crowe decided on a quick strategy that helped endear his lads to the fan base even more than their success, community appearances and overall goodwill had already fostered. "Vic was really smart, and he knew they were lining out of the stadium selling tickets, so he took us out and we warmed up right around the stadium," recalls Willie Anderson. "The response was phenomenal, a memory that I will never forget," says Graham Brown of that lap. Fans were able to shake hands with and encourage the Portland players as they moved slowly around the stadium in one final act of adherence to the community ethos so stressed by Crowe, Leo Crowther and Don Paul.

In a perfect bookend to a remarkable season in Portland, the Timbers closed their home schedule in the rain against the St. Louis Stars in the semifinal at Civic Stadium. One hundred and six days after losing their season opener to rivals the Seattle Sounders, the Portland Timbers had captured the city and been branded the denizens of Soccer City, USA. A total of 33,503 fans ignored the rain. The record crowd outnumbered the overflow audience from five nights earlier and provided tangible evidence that the Timbers were the most important team in town. Mildred Schwab's bleachers were completely filled on August 17, 1975, as excited and anxious supporters came to cheer on their Timbers one last time.

From the opening kickoff, Portland controlled possession, worked its usual avenues and ultimately found a match-winner from its standard-bearer. Behind twenty-eight shots, fifteen of them on frame, the Timbers used Willie

Anderson and Jimmy Kelly to secure the needed advantage. Kelly would have given Portland a greater advantage had his shot not glanced the left post with just eleven minutes to play. Yet it was the crosses, as usual, that ultimately did in the Timbers' opponents.

"We beat them with the wingers. We didn't always develop our drives—the wet field slowed us up—but we took the game to them. We worked the way we wanted to," exclaimed Vic Crowe afterward. By interchanging Kelly and Anderson, flipping them from right to left and back again, Crowe tormented the St. Louis defenders, who were unequal to the task. With passes more difficult to thread through the middle, Crowe also pushed Barry Powell farther up field than usual, creating a 4-2-4 formation at times.

The first half passed without incident, or at least without need for the score sheet, but the second half would not be spared. In the fifty-sixth minute, Brian Godfrey sent a free kick to Powell, who crossed to Graham Day, whose header came to Withe, who nodded in one final Civic Stadium goal. The roar of 33,503 was immense as sopping fans were already discussing travel plans for a weekend in San Jose, site of Soccer Bowl '75.

Still, thirty-five minutes remained before Portlanders could claim a spot in the NASL final. Heroics were in order, and a combination of Grahams kept St. Louis from leveling the score. Graham Brown recorded eleven saves, while Graham Day won MVP honors for the match, both for his assist on Withe's match-winner and for his ability to stop the Stars' high-scoring forwards. St. Louis manager John Sewell tried bringing in six-foot-four John Carenza just after the hour to bring equal height to the Stars' forward line, but it was not enough to find a tying goal. Brown saved twice on hard shots from John Hawley and performed his best trick in stopping Pat McBride off a Hawley cross late in the game. That stop was enough to lift Portland to the Soccer Bowl and led to one more lap of honor.

Rather than a stampede of fans onto the pitch, the response to the climaxing Timbers' season was one of measured respect and appreciation. Knowing a victory lap was in store as the final whistle blew, Portland's fans generously applauded, aware of the fact that it might be the last time they could cheer for the likes of Withe, Anderson or Brown. Though the cheering would not have been mistaken for anything other than joy, a touch of admiration and thanks gave the send-off a different feeling than the quarterfinal eruption. When Barry Lynch finally led the Timbers on that last jaunt around the old ground, a British visitor might have thought it was a reunion game or a testimonial for the entire team.

Timbers and St. Louis Stars players exit the field after Portland's 1–0 victory in the NASL semifinals on August 17 at Civic Stadium. Fans can be seen atop neighboring houses, a necessity for viewing with 33,503 in attendance, then the largest crowd for an NASL playoff game and the largest in league history for a game not featuring Pelé. *Courtesy of Chris Dangerfield, personal collection.*

Tony Betts with city councilwoman Mildred Schwab at a post-game party. Schwab became a close friend of many Timbers players, having taken them out to dinner, arranged for a party with the Joffrey Ballet and even shared cigarettes in the tunnel just before games. *Courtesy of Stella Terry, personal collection.*

Even the players were reminiscent in their post-game comments. Said Ray Martin of the Timbers' arrival in April, "We were optimistic; we knew we would be aggressive enough. We were hoping to persuade the fans to take an interest in us—and in soccer." A veteran of thirteen years at the top of England's Football League, Martin best expressed the sentiment of the seventeen Timbers, but particularly the British contingent, saying, "I think I've had the greatest thrill of my life here." Graham Day, speaking thirty-six years later, agrees: "The best four months of my life."

The final touches of the last game at Civic Stadium were complete when Mildred Schwab entered the dressing room to congratulate her lads. "She's been very emotionally involved with us," Leo Crowther said as the city councilwoman made her way through the Timbers' locker room. "I loved Mildred. She's one of the greatest ladies I've ever met," says Willie Anderson.

THAT PORTLAND AND TAMPA BAY were set to play for the NASL's championship was in one way unique and in another somewhat familiar. Never before had two expansion sides competed in the league's championship game, though in the two previous seasons an expansion team had won the title. The 1975 final was set to follow in step, regardless of the winner.[21] Yet the circumstances of the match were very different. For the first time, the NASL was playing its championship game at a neutral site.

Despite a distance of nearly seven hundred miles, two thousand tickets were allotted to the Timbers organization, while hundreds of other fans purchased packages for organized flights and hotels. Lake Oswego Travel Center, a group that had taken fans on away trips earlier in the season, sold two hundred packages, while Imperial Tour and Travel appealed directly to the so-called Timbers Boosters. Though an official Booster Club was not created until the 1976 season, the group scheduled flights down and back for August 24, the date of Soccer Bowl '75. Still more fans came via Amtrak on overnight cars. The Earthquakes reported at least six hundred room requests from Portlanders at the Hyatt House Hotel, where the Timbers team stayed.

The Timbers themselves planned to remain in Portland until the twenty-third, training under their usual schedule and taking advantage of the week in between the semifinal and the Soccer Bowl. Three games in the previous eight days had left the Timbers in need of a break, though their expectations of a normal week were almost immediately quashed. Due to

TIMBERS
BOOSTERS

*LET'S CHEER OUR TEAM ON TO
THE CHAMPIONSHIP!!*

Here's the schedule on AUGUST 24, 1975

7:45 AM	Check in United Airlines, Portland International Airport
8:30 AM	Depart United breakfast flight #365
10:01 AM	Arrive San Francisco International Airport
10:15 AM	Depart Airport by Private Motorcoach
11:30 AM	Arrive San Jose Stadium
12:00 Noon	CHAMPIONSHIP GAME STARTS!! (reserved seats included)
2:00 to 2:30 PM	Depart (as winners, we hope!) San Jose Stadium
4:00 to 5:00 PM	Arrive San Francisco International Airport (plenty of "watering holes" and restaurant facilities)
5:30 PM	Check in United Airlines, San Francisco International Airport
6:00 PM	Depart United dinner flight #878
8:01 PM	Arrive Portland International Airport

$122.50/person

LIMITED SPACE . . . so come in today

224-8300
IMPERIAL TOUR and TRAVEL INC.
728 S.W. Washington, Portland, Oregon 97205

The group that became the Timbers Booster Club arranged for travel to Soccer Bowl '75 through Imperial Tour and Travel, among other providers. *Courtesy of Chris Dangerfield, personal collection.*

the marketability of a neutral site championship game and a national television broadcast, not to mention the inclusion of Pelé in the league's advertising, the NASL required both clubs to arrive on August 21. Luncheons, a beauty contest and skills clinics were scheduled for the two teams alongside Pelé and Kyle Rote Jr., the league's two biggest names.

Meanwhile, the NASL announced its league All-Star team for the season. Amazingly, not a single Timbers player was included in the first eleven, despite the team finishing the season at the top of the table and reaching the Soccer Bowl. Both Peter Withe, the league's fourth-leading scorer, and Barry Powell made the second team, while Graham Day landed on the Honorable Mention list. Though Portland was focused on winning the championship, the lack of national recognition was hurtful, especially with Pelé, who had played in fewer than ten games, qualifying for the team, seemingly on reputation alone.

As the teams gathered in San Jose with nothing but time until their Sunday championship game, the feelings of each side slowly crept into the reporting newspapers. Though many in Portland seemed sure that the Timbers were the favored team, Tampa Bay manager Eddie Firmani noted that his team's 3–0 win over the Miami Toros in the Eastern semifinal left his team confident and undamaged before the big game. Firmani planned to have his team play as aggressively as its Rowdies nickname suggested, penning the Timbers in on a much smaller field.

For their part, the Timbers, and specifically Vic Crowe, were worried about the size of the pitch. Having played twice in San Jose earlier in the season, Crowe was certain that the sixty-four-yard-wide field would be a factor against the Rowdies. Even recently defeated St. Louis Stars manager

John Sewell expected a different outlook from the Timbers. "Anderson may well give Tampa Bay more than they can handle, unless the narrower pitch helps them cut him off," Sewell said two days before the final.

Back in Portland, arrangements were made to have a reception for the returning Timbers from 9:00 p.m. to 1:00 a.m. on Sunday night the twenty-fourth, regardless of the result of the game. Rather than have the possibility of thousands of fans descending on Portland International Airport, the team set the party for the Hilton Hotel, site of several of the club's post-match receptions during the season.

The day before Soccer Bowl '75, Vic Crowe announced that his team was mostly fit for the game. Tony Betts was likely to miss out, at least on starting, due to the thigh injury that had limited him to a substitute's role in the quarterfinal and left him out entirely during the semifinal. Otherwise, Crowe planned to use the same lineup—with Brian Godfrey in defense and Chris Dangerfield in the midfield—that was used late in the season. Crowe also vowed to keep playing in the same style, not changing his plans just because of the size of the pitch or the opponent. "We're going to take it to them, regardless. We won't lay back and defend. We won't be negative for sixty minutes. No way. We're going to go at them, take the initiative and hopefully get one or two goals," he announced after the team's final practice.

ARSÈNE AUGUSTE IS A NAME that has haunted Timbers players and supporters since August 24, 1975. Though he was unknown prior to kickoff, not even listed on the Tampa Bay Rowdies' roster that day, Auguste scored what turned out to be the match-winner in Soccer Bowl '75. With the game scoreless through the hour, the Haitian international defender came on to replace Malcolm Linton in the sixty-third minute. Three minutes later, Auguste blasted a stunning shot from thirty yards to end the Timbers' dream season.

"We always hated playing in San Jose because it was a really narrow field. It was a football field, so it didn't suit our team and really cut out our effectiveness," says Willie Anderson of the Soccer Bowl. Indeed, the formula suggested by St. Louis manager John Sewell turned into a difficult reality for Portland.

Seattle Sounders manager John Best offered the best explanation of what happened to the Portland Timbers immediately following the game: "It was apparent that Tampa's defense was keyed on stopping Portland's wings. I thought that Withe played a tremendous game, but he didn't have the opportunities in this game because Tampa denied him the complementing play on the wings, particularly Mike Connell on Jimmy Kelly. Willie Anderson gave Tampa a lot of trouble, and I think he helped Firmani make the decision to take Linton out—which was ironic."

Indeed, the Timbers were frustrated on the left side of the field throughout the championship game. Though two thousands fans made the trip south and were vocal in their support of their Timbers, Portland's players finally met a team that matched their speed, physicality and ability. Given just enough luck, too, the Tampa Bay Rowdies were crowned champions of the North American Soccer League.

The Timbers did have chances, however, with Chris Dangerfield nearly opening scoring with a first-half shot that slipped just wide after goalkeeper Paul Hammond got a hand on it. Barry Lynch launched a cracking, thirty-five-yard volley that required another Hammond save, though the Tampa goalkeeper brought out his finest work in a dual save against Barry Powell and Peter Withe midway through the first half.

In Soccer Bowl '75, Chris Dangerfield slide tackles Tampa Bay Rowdies midfielder Mark Lindsay just before Tommy McLaren can make a play on the ball. Despite this fine defensive play, the Timbers fell to the Rowdies 2–0 on August 24 in San Jose. *Courtesy of Chris Dangerfield, personal collection.*

Both sides struggled to maintain possession on the bumpy, poorly kept turf at San Jose's Spartan Stadium, so the game turned toward explosive chances rather than sustained buildup. One such eruption came from the boot of Auguste. The recently inserted defender drifted forward as the Rowdies pushed toward goal, and a Derek Smethurst deflection from a John Sisson shot fell right in Auguste's path. With one touch, he powered a shot toward Graham Brown's goal. Unluckily for the Timbers, the ball caromed downward, off the crossbar and into the goal. "It was one of those shots you whack and pray," Anderson recalls. The goal broke the deadlock and stunned the Timbers.

Withe had a shot saved by Hammond in the seventy-ninth minute, but it was Anderson who came closest to bringing Portland onto the score sheet. With eight minutes left and trailing by a goal, the Timbers' best player of the day found himself clear, having worked his way around the left corner of the Tampa Bay defense. Anderson had Hammond beaten, but his would-be equalizer ricocheted off the post.

Five minutes later, the Rowdies secured the championship. With Portland pushing defenders forward, looking for a last-second equalizer, Clyde Best corralled a through ball from Smethurst, sprinted past Graham Day and poked in the second goal, eluding an onrushing Graham Brown. That goal in the eighty-eighth minute ended the game and the hopes of the Portland Timbers.

The Portland Timbers

Just as quickly as it all came together, the 1975 Portland Timbers season came to a close. The team boarded a bus, drove to Oakland and took a plane directly back to Portland. From PDX, the players and coaches were taken to the Hilton Hotel, where six hundred disappointed but spirited supporters greeted them. Vic Crowe led the crowd in cheers, though he did not exactly promise to return for 1976, saying, "I want you to know that I want to do the very best to keep the Timber situation as good and exciting as it was this first season."

After several players and general manager Don Paul spoke, the team departed for the Tall Firs apartment complex for the last time. On Monday morning, August 25, ten Timbers players boarded a flight back to London as the breakup of the team began. Having sparred with English managers and the Football League, Crowe's loan agreements seemed destined to prevent a full returning team for the '76 season, despite the overwhelming success in the debut year.

Willie Anderson and Graham Day both immediately left Portland as their home clubs, Cardiff City and Bristol Rovers, respectively, were set to play each other on the twenty-sixth in the 1975–76 English League Cup second round. The next day, Tommy McLaren's Port Vale played away against Hereford United in the League Cup. It was almost as if the Timbers season had not happened at all. Yet, in other ways, it was only just the beginning of the Timbers' story. The 1975–76 League Cup final saw Willie Donachie assist on the match-winner for Manchester City against Pat Howard and

Newcastle United. Howard joined the Portland Timbers on loan from Birmingham City in 1978, while Donachie joined the Timbers in 1980 and played three seasons in Portland.

Crowe's mishandling of the loan agreements and his departure from Portland without a contract for the 1976 season kept fans waiting through the winter. Crowe eventually agreed to return to Portland, though with several thousand dollars less to his name, after a hefty fine came down from the NASL office. His return also came without some of the biggest names from the debut season of 1975. Willie Anderson, Graham Day, Tommy McLaren, Peter Withe, Barry Powell, Barry Lynch, Graham Brown and Donald Gardner all failed to return through various circumstances. The effects were evident in '76, when after winning four of its first six games, Portland lost five straight, including 3–0 to the New York Cosmos in front of 32,247 at Civic Stadium. Nine more losses followed, and the Timbers finished their second season with just eight victories.

From there, the Timbers rebuilt through a difficult 1977 season and were a top club in 1978. New manager Don Megson came to Portland from Bristol Rovers and brought in players from areas outside the West Midlands. He brought Portland again to the NASL's semifinal round before bowing out 6–0 on aggregate to Franz Beckenbauer's Cosmos.

Portland entered into an agreement with Nike in 1979, wearing the local shoe company's jerseys, tracksuits and shoes, marking the Timbers as the first soccer club in the world to be so outfitted. The new kits did nothing to stop a poor season though, and the Timbers rejoined the league's bottom-feeders. Local timber company Louisiana Pacific purchased the club from Oregon Soccer, Inc. ahead of the 1980 season and promised bigger and better things from the Timbers. Megson purchased big-name players like Donachie and Dutch star Robbie Rensenbrink. Yet seven losses in their first eleven matches, including a 5–1 destruction at the hands of the California Surf and just three goals from Rensenbrink, led to Megson's sacking.

Crowe was brought out of retirement after general manager Peter Warner coached the team for three games. Brian Gant's goal against the Atlanta Chiefs assured Crowe of a victory in his return match, yet the Timbers' five-game winning streak to close the season could do nothing to prevent a last-place finish in the National Conference's Western Division in 1980.

In 1981, with Crowe back at the helm for a full season, Portland managed to reach the playoffs for the third time, earning a best-of-three series with the Western Division champion San Diego Sockers. The Timbers forced a third game but lost to San Diego, ending their NASL-era's playoff history.

Portland returned for the 1982 season, ultimately its last, finishing with a 14-18 record and losing its final game 1–0 to the Seattle Sounders at Civic Stadium. That bookend was appropriate, as the once-proud Timbers were folded and the remaining players dispersed among rivals or left to retirement.

Despite an eight-year run in the North American Soccer League, the Timbers were never able to recapture the magic of that summer of '75. Willie Anderson, Graham Day, Graham Brown, Barry Powell and Barry Lynch all returned eventually, with Anderson and Day emerging as club legends. Yet without that successful first season, there might never have been a second, third or eighth season for the Timbers. Dozens of clubs were founded and folded during Portland's run, so it is safe to suggest that only the enormous popularity of the original Timbers kept the club afloat as long as they managed.

The Timbers' name reemerged in 1989 when longtime fan Art Dixon purchased the name from the then-defunct NASL and renamed his FC Portland club. Playing first in the Western Soccer League and in 1990 in the American Professional Soccer League, the Timbers' name and colors once again represented professional soccer at Civic Stadium. The likes of Kasey Keller and Scott Benedetti played under player-coach John Bain, a Scottish midfielder who joined the NASL version of the Timbers in 1978 and became the club's all-time leading goal scorer.

After two years, the Timbers again folded, leaving eleven years before a Timbers team graced the artificial pitch in downtown Portland. In 2001, Portland Family Entertainment created a team in a joint business model with minor-league baseball, bringing the Portland Timbers back into professional soccer. Their colors were the same, but the logo was different for several years before popular sentiment required ownership to return the famous circular crest. These Timbers played in the A-League, one step below Major League Soccer's top flight.

In 2004, the A-League changed names to the United Soccer League's first division, though the Timbers remained a tier below MLS. Gavin Wilkinson, Scot Thompson, Alan Gordon and Byron Alvarez led the Timbers to their best season in the second division, winning the Commissioner's Cup trophy as the league's top team. But the Timbers crashed out of the playoffs, falling 3–2 on aggregate to the Seattle Sounders in the quarterfinal round, a cruel reversal of the most famous game in Timbers' history twenty-nine years earlier.

Portland again crested in 2009 as the second division's top team, winning a second Commissioner's Cup and earning a bye to the semifinal round of the playoffs. Yet a 5–4 aggregate loss to the Vancouver Whitecaps kept Portland from reaching its first final since 1975, again leaving the inaugural season as the best ever for any team called the Timbers.

After ten seasons in the second division, the Portland Timbers returned to the top flight of American soccer when they debuted in Major League Soccer on March 19, 2011, against the Colorado Rapids. Though the Timbers suffered a 3–1 defeat in their MLS opener, Portland again found success at home in front of the Timbers Army, the supporters group built during the second division days. Thirty-six years after their first tilt, fans of the Portland Timbers name, brand and history poured into the newly renamed Jeld-Wen Field to witness the home side defeat the Chicago Fire, 4–2, on April 14, 2011.

From involvement in the development of the soccer apparel industry to the founding of youth clubs and collegiate programs, the original Timbers have had an immense impact on Portland far beyond their first four months. Several players returned to the Rose City to spend significant parts of their lives in the city and are involved with the current manifestation of the club. That connection to the earliest days of the Timbers is an invaluable part of what makes Portland Soccer City, USA.

Notes

CHAPTER 1

1. Both the *Oregonian* and the *Oregon Journal* misname the coaching candidates on multiple occasions. Gordon Jaco, Gordon Goodwin and Gordon Crowe were all names that found their way into the published pages of the local newspapers. Only upon Crowe's hiring was his name corrected.

2. Gordon Jago only stayed at Millwall through the 1976–77 season, after which he moved back to the United States to manage the Tampa Bay Rowdies. Freddie Goodwin came to the NASL in 1976 to be the first manager of the Minnesota Kicks.

3. NASL rules were different for expansion teams and existing teams in 1975. Returning clubs were required to have at least five North American players, while the five new teams needed just three such players.

4. The Portland Beavers moved into Multnomah Stadium in 1956 after fifty-one years of baseball at Vaughn Street Park in Northwest Portland. The first Tartan turf was installed at Civic Stadium in 1969 to accommodate both the baseball team and American football games.

CHAPTER 2

5. Bernie Fagan joined the Timbers ahead of the 1980 season. He played in Portland for the Timbers' final three years in the NASL, 1980–82, before

retiring and starting a coaching career that has included FC Portland, Warner Pacific University, Portland State University and various youth camps and teams.

6. Mike Flater moved to the Timbers early in 1978 after starting the year with the Oakland Stompers. Scoring seven goals in his twenty-two games, Flater was one of the keys to Portland's second semifinal appearance. He stayed with the Timbers through the 1980 season.

CHAPTER 3

7. In 1969, the NASL split its season into two parts. The first saw British clubs playing under NASL club names: Aston Villa as Atlanta Chiefs, West Ham United as Baltimore Bays, Dundee United as Dallas Tornado, Wolverhampton Wanderers as Kansas City Spurs and Kilmarnock as St. Louis Stars. Future Timbers Willie Anderson, Brian Godfrey, Barry Lynch and Brian Tiler (1976) played in Atlanta that summer. The second half of the season had the regulars back for the five-team NASL, including Chiefs defender Vic Crowe.

8. A term like "holding midfielder" did not exist in 1975. This terminology will be used throughout sections devoted to tactics, as it is more difficult to identify players by their contemporary titles. For example, in an interview with Willie Anderson, he referred to himself at Aston Villa as an "outside right" when playing against left back Ray Martin at Birmingham City. Left back translates easily enough, but outside right is a holdover from older formations featuring three, four or five forwards.

9. For a more in-depth look at the Timbers' tactics across the 1975 season, see "First Time Around," an article in issue zero of the *Blizzard*.

10. San Jose State dates its program to 1927, and the Earthquakes' backup goalkeeper in 1975 was Spartan star Gary St. Clair.

11. Archie Roboostoff joined the Timbers in 1977, playing twenty-three games and scoring four goals before being traded to the Oakland Stompers three games into the 1978 season.

CHAPTER 4

12. Eusébio starred at Benfica and for Portugal through the 1960s and early '70s. He retired from Benfica and moved to the Boston Minutemen in

1975. He played three seasons in the NASL, including 1976 with the Toronto Metros-Croatia, which he led to Soccer Bowl '76.

13. Jinky Johnstone was a member of the Celtic's "Lisbon Lions," winners of the 1967 European Cup. In 2002, Hoops supporters named him the greatest Celtic player who ever lived.

14. Gardner was the youngest player, born on August 30, 1955, making him exactly three weeks younger than Dangerfield.

Chapter 5

15. Henry McCully scored the Americans' only full international goal of 1975 in a 3–1 loss to Costa Rica.

16. The Cosmos moved back to Yankee Stadium to accommodate larger crowds in 1976, though the average attendance, 18,227, was less than the 22,500 capacity at Downing Stadium.

17. Future Timber Pat McMahon scored the opening goal of Aston Villa's 2–1 victory over Santos on February 21, 1972. Mick Hoban made his first team debut for Villa and was given Pelé's shirt after the match.

18. At the time of publication, the Portland Timbers have had two Hermann Trophy award winners play on their teams. The first was Glenn Myernick, who won the award in 1976. The second was Darlington Nagbe, the Timbers' top draft choice ahead of their 2011 season in Major League Soccer.

Chapter 6

19. Several Welsh clubs play in the English Football League, including Cardiff City, Swansea City, Newport County and Wrexham.

20. Hank Liotart was traded to Portland ten games into the 1976 season. He spent the rest of '76 and the entire 1977 campaign in Portland before leaving the Northwest for the San Diego Sockers.

Chapter 7

21. The Minnesota Kicks nearly gave expansion teams four consecutive titles, ultimately losing to Toronto Metros-Croatia in Soccer Bowl '76.

Bibliography

Interviews

Willie Anderson, Tony Betts, Graham Brown, Don Cox, Leo Crowther, Gisele Currier, Chris Dangerfield, Scott Daniels, Graham Day, Art Dixon, Bernie Fagan, Terry Fisher, Roger Goldingay, Linda Hoban, Mick Hoban, Vic Karsner, Jimmy Kelly, Dave Landry, Ray Martin, Nick Nicolas, Dennis O'Meara, John Polis, Barry Powell, Augusto and Beatriz Proaño, Jim Rilatt, Kurt Schubothe, Gary St. Clair, Dave Stoops, Jim Taylor, Stella Terry, Bob Wilmot and Peter Withe

Newspapers/Magazines

Berkshire Eagle
Blizzard, issue zero
Daily Journal of Commerce
Los Angeles Times
New York Times
Oregon Historical Quarterly (Summer 2011)
Oregonian
Oregon Journal
Sports Illustrated

Books

Dure, Beau. *Long-Range Goals: The Success Story of Major League Soccer*. Dulles, VA: Potomac, 2010.

Tossell, David. *Playing for Uncle Sam: The Brits' Story of the North American Soccer League*. Edinburgh, Scotland: Mainstream Publishing, 2003.

Wilson, Jonathan. *Inverting the Pyramid: A History of Football Tactics*. London: Orion, 2008.

Other Publications

Leo Crowther autobiography (unfinished at time of publication)

New York City Department of Parks and Recreation. *The African American Experience.*

1975 *Portland City Directory*

2009 *San Jose State University Men's Soccer Media Guide*

Websites

North American Soccer League Jerseys, http://www.NASLJerseys.com

Portland Timbers Fan Page, http://www.TimbersFanPage.com

Zonal Marking, http://www.ZonalMarking.net

Index

A

A-League 114
Alvarez, Byron 114
American Professional Soccer League
     114
Anderson, Willie 19, 22, 24, 30, 36, 38,
     39, 41, 42, 43, 45, 47, 53, 54,
     55, 56, 59, 64, 66, 68, 69, 74,
     76, 77, 82, 83, 84, 85, 87, 89,
     93, 95, 98, 102, 104, 105, 107,
     109, 110, 111, 112, 113, 114
Andrews, Jimmy 93
Aston Villa 11, 15, 17, 19, 20, 33, 38,
     40, 83
Atlanta Apollos. *See* Atlanta Chiefs
Atlanta Chiefs 11, 15, 17, 19, 113
Auguste, Arsène 109, 111
Augustino, Rino 21

B

Bain, John 114
Baldwin, Tommy 96, 97
Baltimore Bays 14
Baltimore Comets 11, 71, 76
Bandov, Boris 48, 93, 94
Banhoffer, Uri 55, 57, 68, 69

Batie, Don 53
Beckenbauer, Franz 113
Benedetti, Scott 114
Benson Hotel 45, 60
Berg, Dick 13
Best, Clyde 111
Best, John 91, 96, 109
Betts, Tony 20, 22, 24, 28, 32, 33, 36,
     37, 39, 40, 42, 43, 45, 46, 47,
     48, 49, 52, 57, 66, 68, 70, 74,
     76, 78, 79, 82, 86, 93, 98, 102,
     109
Bilecki, Željko 35
Birmingham City 14, 19, 54, 77, 84,
     89, 113
Blackmore, Richard 37
Blanco, Sergio 53
Blitz Beer 45
Bonetti, Peter 9, 87
Boston Minutemen 11, 75, 76, 96
Bristol Rovers 17, 20, 112, 113
Brown, Graham 19, 30, 33, 35, 36,
     42, 43, 48, 57, 59, 66, 68, 76,
     82, 86, 89, 93, 95, 97, 101, 104,
     105, 111, 113, 114

C

California Surf 113
Calloway, Laurie 58, 92
Cardiff City 19, 22, 36, 38, 93, 112
Carenza, John 87, 105
Carr, Dick 40, 78, 80, 81, 82
Catlin Gabel School 21, 37
Cawston, Mervyn 43
Chicago Fire 115
Chicago Sting 40, 85, 99
Child, Paul 59
Civic Stadium 9, 16, 24, 26, 27, 28, 35,
        36, 40, 42, 43, 44, 51, 53, 60,
        64, 75, 78, 92, 95, 98, 99, 100,
        101, 104, 105, 107, 113, 114
Clemenica, Reggie 74
Clough, Brian 40
Coker, Ade 76
Colorado Rapids 115
Columbia Cup 46, 47, 66
Commissioner's Cup 114
Connell, Mike 110
Cooper, Ken 52
Counce, Dan 48
Cox, Don 28
Craig, Derek 48, 93
Creamer, Peter 51
Crossley, Paul 90, 97, 101
Crowe, Vic 14, 15, 16, 17, 18, 19, 20,
        21, 22, 23, 24, 25, 28, 29, 31,
        33, 34, 35, 36, 37, 38, 39, 40,
        42, 43, 44, 45, 46, 47, 49, 53,
        54, 55, 56, 57, 58, 59, 60, 63,
        64, 66, 67, 68, 69, 70, 72, 74,
        75, 77, 78, 82, 83, 84, 86, 87,
        88, 91, 93, 94, 95, 97, 98, 99,
        102, 103, 104, 105, 108, 109,
        112, 113
Crowther, Leo 15, 16, 18, 19, 20, 21,
        22, 23, 28, 31, 33, 34, 48, 49,
        64, 68, 72, 77, 78, 79, 80, 81,
        82, 83, 104, 107
Culp, Ron 46, 54, 55, 72, 78, 79

D

Daggatt, Walt 12, 29
Dallas Tornado 12, 49, 50, 51, 84, 85
Dangerfield, Chris 19, 23, 24, 28, 30,
        31, 33, 35, 45, 54, 57, 58, 59,
        61, 63, 66, 67, 68, 69, 76, 86,
        88, 93, 99, 101, 102, 109, 110
Davies, Geoff 76
Day, Graham 9, 20, 22, 24, 35, 37, 38,
        39, 40, 43, 47, 48, 52, 54, 56,
        57, 59, 66, 72, 74, 86, 93, 94,
        95, 97, 98, 105, 107, 108, 111,
        112, 113, 114
Delta Park 25, 26
Denver Dynamos 11, 17, 36
Derby County 40
Dillon Stadium 71, 74
Dixon, Art 114
Dixon, Joe 103
Donachie, Willie 112, 113
Doncaster Rovers 19, 89
Downing Stadium 78, 80, 81, 82

E

Easton, Jim 66
Empire Stadium 38
England, Mike 91, 96, 97, 101
Eusébio 51, 76, 77

F

Fagan, Bernie 28
FC Portland 114
Firmani, Eddie 110
Fisher, Terry 56, 69
Foulkes, Bill 42, 43, 44
Francis Field 85, 86
Fuente, Luis de la 82

G

Gabriel, Jimmy 28, 90, 91, 96
Gardner, Donald 20, 24, 30, 31, 35,
        36, 49, 54, 56, 58, 61, 63, 74,
        76, 90, 91, 93, 113

Gavrić, Gabbo 48
Gerber Advertising Agency 16
Gidman, John 22
Gilbertson, John 12, 13, 26, 30, 85, 98
Gillett, Dave 90, 91
Godfrey, Brian 17, 18, 22, 24, 29, 30,
        35, 36, 39, 40, 41, 42, 43, 46,
        49, 51, 52, 54, 56, 57, 59, 60,
        64, 66, 67, 69, 72, 82, 83, 86,
        90, 93, 94, 95, 96, 98, 99, 101,
        102, 105, 109
Goldingay, Roger 21, 23, 33, 45, 54,
        55, 59, 72, 74, 98, 99, 102
Goldschmidt, Neil 23
Goodwin, Freddie 14, 77, 84, 89
Gordon, Alan 114
Graydon, Ray 40
Greco, Peter 39, 66
Griffiths, Arfon 102

H

Hammond, Paul 110, 111
Harper, Don 30
Hartford Bicentennials 67, 71, 72, 73,
        74
Hawley, John 86, 105
Hill, Gordon 43, 44
Hoban, Linda 18, 22, 30, 32
Hoban, Mick 17, 21, 22, 25, 27, 28,
        30, 32, 33, 35, 39, 42, 45, 46,
        49, 54, 55, 61, 64, 66, 69, 72,
        83, 86, 89, 93, 97, 98, 101
Horton, Randy 81
Howard, Pat 112
Hunt, Lamar 12, 13, 50

I

Ivanow, Mike 48, 93

J

Jackson, Albert 52
Jago, Gordon 14
Janduda, Józef 41
Jefferson County Stadium 36

Jijon, Ed 42
Johnson, Glen 47
Johnstone, Jinky 58, 59

K

Kaiser Chiefs 37
KATU TV 40, 78, 81, 100, 104
Keller, Kasey 114
Kelly, Jimmy 19, 23, 29, 30, 31, 35, 36,
        38, 39, 42, 52, 54, 56, 57, 60,
        61, 63, 64, 66, 69, 74, 76, 87,
        90, 91, 93, 96, 100, 102, 105,
        110
KOIN radio 34, 104
Krazy George 48

L

Lamptey, George 41
Landry, Dave 21, 23, 33, 55, 98, 99
Lees, Terry 59
Lenarduzzi, Sam 66
Linton, Malcolm 109
Liotart, Hank 96
Los Angeles Aztecs 11, 14, 21, 55, 56,
        68, 69, 76, 97, 99, 103
Louisiana Pacific 113
Lynch, Barry 19, 28, 35, 39, 43, 44,
        52, 53, 66, 72, 87, 89, 93, 102,
        105, 110, 113, 114

M

Mackay, Dave 40
Major League Soccer 115
Manchester City 112
Manchester United 19, 38, 42
Manfred Schellscheidt 72
Martin, Ray 19, 28, 30, 35, 39, 43, 49,
        54, 66, 67, 69, 77, 82, 86, 89,
        90, 93, 98, 100, 103, 107
Matteson, Bob 87
McBride, Pat 105
McCully, Charlie 73
McCully, Henry 73
McGarry, Bill 77, 84

McLaren, Tommy 19, 30, 35, 36, 37, 39, 43, 48, 52, 57, 76, 82, 83, 84, 86, 87, 91, 93, 95, 96, 98, 101, 102, 112, 113
McMillan, Doug 56
Megson, Don 113
Memorial Stadium 96, 102
Messing, Shep 76
Miami Toros 56, 71, 108
Michniewski, Jan 76
Middlesbrough FC 51
Millwall 15, 43
Mitchell, Brian 39
Mitić, Ilija 47, 48, 49, 59
Montréal Olympique 11
Mount Hood 68
Multnomah Athletic Club 25, 26
Murdock Stadium 56, 99

N

National Professional Soccer League 11, 14, 85
Newcastle United 113
Newman, Ron 52
Newport County 17
New York Cosmos 51, 69, 77, 78, 81, 113
New York Generals 14
Ngcobo, Shaka 37
Nickerson Field 75, 77
Nicolas, Nick 21, 44, 47, 55, 61, 68, 71, 72, 86, 98, 99, 102
Nolen, John 30
Ntsoelengoe, Ace 37
Nusum, Sam 82, 83

O

Oakland Clippers 74
Odoi, Frank 42
O'Meara, Dennis 16, 18, 52, 64, 72
Ord, Tommy 42
Oregon Soccer, Inc. 12, 13, 14, 15, 26, 30, 35

P

Packwood, Bob 22
Pasero, George 25
Paul, Don 12, 13, 14, 18, 19, 22, 23, 26, 49, 52, 77, 78, 84, 89, 93, 104, 112
Pelé 51, 77, 78, 81, 82, 83, 92, 108
Perri, Ardo 41, 42
Philadelphia Atoms 50, 71, 84, 96, 99
Pisani, John 87
Polis, John 25, 64
Pollock, Don 30
Portland Beavers 75
Portland Family Entertainment 114
Portland Mavericks 27, 75
Portland Storm 12, 26, 75
Portland Thunder 75, 92
Portland Trail Blazers 45, 78
Port Vale 19, 112
Powell, Barry 9, 19, 29, 31, 35, 36, 37, 39, 43, 52, 54, 57, 58, 61, 63, 64, 66, 77, 84, 85, 88, 91, 93, 97, 101, 105, 108, 110, 113, 114
Prefontaine, Steve 43
Proaño, Doc 14
Putnam, Pat 96

R

Rensenbrink, Robbie 113
Renshaw, Mike 52
Revie, Don 51
Rhode Island Oceaneers 72
Rigby, Bob 96
Rilatt, Bernie 30, 84
Rilatt, Jim 84
Roboostoff, Archie 48
Rochester Lancers 40, 41, 71
Rote, Kyle, Jr. 50, 51, 52, 108
Rowlands, John 96, 97, 101
Russell, Alex 57

S

San Antonio Thunder 49, 53, 56, 98
San Diego Sockers 113

San Jose Earthquakes 11, 14, 21, 47, 49, 57, 59, 92
Schubothe, Kurt 29
Schwab, Mildred 9, 26, 27, 104, 107
Seattle Sounders 11, 14, 16, 21, 26, 28, 71, 81, 84, 89, 90, 92, 95, 96, 97, 98, 99, 100, 101, 102, 103, 104, 109, 114
Seerey, Mike 86
Sewell, John 85, 98, 105, 109
Shewsbury Town 92
Short, Peter 37
Sibbald, Bobby 99
Siega, Jorge 81
Simões, António 76
Sisson, John 111
Smethurst, Derek 111
Soccer Bowl '75 10, 95, 103, 105, 107, 109
Soccer City, USA 10, 89, 92, 103, 104, 115
Spartan Stadium 47, 48, 49, 58, 111
Sportclub Germania 25
St. Clair, Gary 59, 94
St. Louis Stars 9, 71, 85, 87, 98, 99, 103, 104, 105, 108
Sühnholz, Wolfgang 76

T

Tall Firs Apartment Complex 23, 31, 45, 112
Tampa Bay Rowdies 67, 71, 107, 109, 110, 111
Tartan turf 9, 24, 27, 28, 33, 35, 36, 39, 42, 54, 69
Taylor, John 57, 69, 99
Terry, Stella 61
Thompson, Scot 114
Timber Creek Apartment Complex 23, 31
Timbers Booster Club 61
Toplak, Ivan 48, 95
Toronto Metros 21, 35
Toronto Metros-Croatia 35, 71
Tryout 20, 21, 98
Twamley, Bruce 66

U

United Soccer Association 11, 85
United Soccer Leagues 114

V

Vancouver Whitecaps 11, 14, 37, 39, 40, 46, 47, 60, 63, 66, 71, 99, 115
Veee, Juli 57, 69

W

Warner, Peter 113
Washington Diplomats 11, 71
Watling, Barry 29, 91, 94, 101, 102
Webb, John 43
Weber, Greg 47
Webster, Adrian 96
Welch, Art 48
Welsh, Kevin 73
Western Soccer League 114
Wicks, Clarence 30
Wilkinson, Gavin 114
Wilson, Jonathan 40
Wilson, Les 46
Withe, Peter 10, 19, 24, 30, 35, 37, 39, 42, 43, 47, 48, 53, 57, 58, 59, 64, 69, 70, 74, 77, 78, 82, 84, 85, 86, 89, 91, 93, 94, 95, 96, 98, 101, 102, 105, 108, 110, 111, 113
Wolverhampton Wanderers 19, 20, 23, 31, 53, 63, 77, 91
Wooler, Alan 76
Woosnam, Phil 11, 13, 14, 84, 92, 95
Wrexham FC 22, 36

Z

Zanatta, Sergio 39, 46

About the Author

Michael Orr is managing writer and editor at FC Media, LLC, in Portland, Oregon, and is a freelance soccer writer and podcast host. A shared love of history and soccer has led to articles published in the *Blizzard*, the *Oregon Historical Quarterly* and numerous blogs.